Projects & Techniques for
metal clay
JEWELRY

Projects & Techniques for
metal clay
JEWELRY

A Creative Approach to Making 13 Bracelets,
Necklaces, Earrings, Findings & More

Tamara Honaman

Other Schiffer Craft Books on Related Subjects:

Mastering Contemporary Jewelry Design: Inspiration, Process, and Finding Your Voice, Loretta Lam, ISBN 978-0-7643-5919-4

Polymer Clay Jewelry: The Art of Caning, Mathilde Brun, ISBN 978-0-7643-4456-5

Weaving with Wire: Creating Woven Metal Fabric, Christine K. Miller, ISBN 978-0-7643-6693-2

Copyright © 2025 by Tamara Honaman

Library of Congress Control Number: 2024953133

All rights reserved. No part of this work may be reproduced or used in any form or by any means—graphic, electronic, or mechanical, including photocopying or information storage and retrieval systems—without written permission from the publisher.

The scanning, uploading, and distribution of this book or any part thereof via the Internet or any other means without the permission of the publisher is illegal and punishable by law. Please purchase only authorized editions and do not participate in or encourage the electronic piracy of copyrighted materials.

"Schiffer Craft" and the crane logo are registered trademarks of Schiffer Publishing, Ltd.

Designed by Lori Malkin Ehrlich
Cover design by Lori Malkin Ehrlich
Type set in Museo Slab / Basic Sans

Photographer: Richard K. Honaman, Jr.
Photo Stylist: Lori Wenger
Photographer (Projects): Jason Masters

ISBN: 978-0-7643-6960-5

ePub: 978-1-5073-0621-5

Printed in China

10 9 8 7 6 5 4 3 2 1

Published by Schiffer Craft
An imprint of Schiffer Publishing, Ltd.
4880 Lower Valley Road
Atglen, PA 19310
Phone: (610) 593-1777; Fax: (610) 593-2002
Email: Info@schifferbooks.com
Web: www.schifferbooks.com

For our complete selection of fine books on this and related subjects, please visit our website at www.schifferbooks.com. You may also write for a free catalog.

Schiffer Publishing's titles are available at special discounts for bulk purchases for sales promotions or premiums. Special editions, including personalized covers, corporate imprints, and excerpts, can be created in large quantities for special needs. For more information, contact the publisher.

We are always looking for people to write books on new and related subjects. If you have an idea for a book, please contact us at proposals@schifferbooks.com.

NOTE: *Fine-silver metal clay is used for the projects in this book. Follow manufacturer's guidelines and warnings accordingly. You can use other metal clays for all projects, adjusted according to brand and manufacturer's recommendations. Use appropriate safety measures and tools accordingly.*

To Rich, Kevin, and Ryan.
You are my world. My everything.
Without you, this book would not exist.

116

122

72

136

Contents

About the Author | **10**   Foreword | **11**   Introduction | **12**

Tools, Materials, and Techniques

CHAPTER 1: TOOLS and MATERIALS | **16**
Metal Clay | **16**
Basic Setup | **17**
Thickness Guides/Gauges | **19**
Tools for Refining the Surface: Wet Clay | **19**
Texture Tools | **20**
Cutting Tools | **20**
Tools for Forming Wet Clay | **21**
Tools for Refining the Surface: Dry Clay | **22**
Firing | **22**
Safety Equipment | **24**
Polishing the Surface | **24**

CHAPTER 2: TECHNIQUES | **26**
Fresh Out of the Package | **27**
Drying Before Its Time | **35**
Working with (Intentionally) Dried Clay | **36**
Coloring Outside the (Clay) Box | **40**
Taking Matters into Your Own Hands | **43**
Finishing | **53**

Projects

CHAPTER 3: Textured Earrings | **60**
CHAPTER 4: Two-Hole Button | **66**
CHAPTER 5: Molded Button with Shank | **72**
CHAPTER 6: Layered Bracelet Link | **78**
CHAPTER 7: Wrapped Tube Bead and Bail | **86**
CHAPTER 8: Masked Textured Pendant | **92**
CHAPTER 9: Large Hook Bracelet | **98**
CHAPTER 10: Toggle Clasp | **104**
CHAPTER 11: Molded Shell Pendant | **110**
CHAPTER 12: Seed Pod Earrings | **116**
CHAPTER 13: Hollow Lentil Earrings | **122**
CHAPTER 14: Abstract Brooch | **130**
CHAPTER 15: Circle Chain Links | **136**

Acknowledgments | **144**

122

86

92

78

98

72

104

66

116

60

136

110

130

About the Author

Tamara Honaman is a passionate jewelry artist who loves teaching and sharing her knowledge with others. She can be found virtually as well as nationally and internationally, teaching, demonstrating, and speaking about making and the business behind being a maker. Tamara's work and projects can be seen in magazines, books, and television programs. She also appears in videos on various industry websites, where she enthusiastically shares her love for all kinds of art materials.

Tamara believes everyone can make something beautiful, and she pours her heart into all she shares. Realizing not everyone learns the same way, she works closely with each person to ensure they can be successful in executing a technique.

Getting her start as editor of "Step by Step" inside *Lapidary Journal Jewelry Artist*, Tamara went on to become the founding editor of *Step-by-Step Beads* along with other *Step-by-Step* magazine titles. Later, she served as the editor of Beading Daily and *Beadwork* magazine and eventually oversaw the Interweave Group as Executive Director.

Building on the success of the long-running Bead Fest shows, which she played a key role in bringing to life, Tamara continues to channel her passion for uniting makers. She now hosts "Heart & Hands of a Maker," an interview-style podcast that spotlights artists from diverse mediums, sharing their stories to inspire and uplift fellow creatives on their journey. Tamara also fosters her own private maker community, where she shares her creative process, works with materials that spark her imagination, and offers techniques to support and empower other makers.

Tamara is certified in various metal clay programs and is a passionate supporter of all metal clay brands and types. She has authored several instructional videos and books, including *Secrets to Metal Clay Success* and *Secrets to Art Clay Success*. She also coauthored *Polymer Clay Master Class*.

Tamara has contributed her expertise as a technical editor for numerous metal clay and jewelry-making publications and held the position of Executive Director of the International Polymer Clay Guild. Tamara has also served on the boards of various jewelry-related organizations.

Foreword

How new is metal clay? Very. It arrived on the scene in the 1990s. More than a quarter century is significant in the life of a single human being, but no more than a speck in the millennia that we humans have been learning to work with metals and clays.

Consisting of metal particles in a clay-like binder, metal clay is in a class by itself, as much hybrid technique as material. As with clay, you can mold metal clay into form, and once formed, you fire it. Unlike firing clay, though, firing metal clay burns off the clay-like substance. What's left is the form in metal, which you finish using metalworking techniques.

In this thoughtful, well-illustrated guide, author Tamara Honaman draws on decades of experience as a creative artisan and dedicated instructor to introduce you to this remarkable material, setting out basic tools and techniques and a host of excellent tips, all conveniently arranged and easy to find again. The fundamentals are followed by eye-catching and progressively more challenging practice projects, with tempting prompts to help you launch your own design ideas.

There is never any time like the present, and this is truly a rare moment in craft history. Thirty-plus years of expert experimentation now make learning to use metal clay easily within reach, yet its potential is still so unexplored. What an extraordinary opportunity to learn something new to you and, just maybe, to discover something new to the world.

— Merle White
Former Editor-in-Chief, Lapidary Journal Jewelry Artist

Introduction

Metal clay is one of the most innovative materials of our present time. It was developed in the 1990s by scientists at Mitsubishi Materials Corporation and Aida Corporation; both were granted patents in 1994.

Original testing was done with 24K gold particles (recycled from scraps left over from microchip manufacturing), a plant-based organic binder, and water. The clay-like material they created was moldable and able to be sculpted, textured, and more. Through testing, progress was made, and the metal used changed to .999 fine silver. The brand Precious Metal Clay (Mitsubishi Materials Corporation) was brought to the United States in 1995. Art Clay Silver (Aida Corporation) was sold primarily in Europe until its United States debut around 1997.

From this innovation and the international launch, guilds were formed, conferences were held, and local chapters and organizations sprung up. Education was spread through print media, through video, and at in-person workshops held the world over. Metal clay was successfully embraced and became part of the jewelry-making fabric.

As feedback came in, new metal clay types and formulas were developed to suit the requests. New types included a paste for joining pieces together, syringe for "writing and drawing," and paper or sheet-type, which could be used like paper, including origami art. The new formulas allowed for quicker drying time, quicker firing time, lower firing temperature options, and less shrinkage.

Since the launch and those early days, the original patent has expired, and the original guilds faded away. BUT! New metal clays and new brands have emerged. Gold and fine silver are still being manufactured along with sterling silver, bronze, copper, brass, and other "base" metals. A new alliance has been formed—AMCAW. This organization embraces all metal clay types and brands, and they welcome all who want to work with the clay, no matter where you started your journey. Other jewelry-making guilds and forums are also embracing this amazing material. It is the best of times.

MY INSPIRATION

Through teaching and working with those I've been fortunate to have in my workshops, I realized any design can be made if you have a handle on the fundamentals of the material. Then it is just a matter of practice and putting the parts and pieces together. I love inspiring others to try a new-to-them material, light their spark, then watch all they create come to life.

This book is written to light your spark. The pages will walk you through the fundamentals of working with metal clay, covering techniques you'll find used throughout the projects. The projects start out a little more straightforward, then increase in complexity. I don't feel the projects are too complicated, but they do get more challenging as you go. That said, you can dive in at the end and pick and choose what design excites you. In my workshops, there are no rules except to work smartly, so you don't hurt yourself or others.

There are many ways you can approach the material I share; what I put forward is based on nearly thirty years of experience, information gathered from the other artists and instructors, and things I've learned working in other disciplines and with other materials. I hope you find it all helpful.

My greatest wish is that you try some or all of these projects, then take them to new heights. There is so much room for advancement and creativity.

PLEASE NOTE: All designs are made using Art Clay Silver fine-silver metal clay. This allowed for consistency in designing, firing, finishing, and presenting the materials. By following manufacturer's instructions, you can adapt these designs to suit any brand or other metal clay type.

Tools, Materials, and Techniques

CHAPTER 1
Tools and Materials

METAL CLAY

Metal clay is a material composed of microscopic particles of metal, an organic plant-based binder, and water. In its fresh state, it is pliable, squishable, and moldable and adapts to forming, texturing, layering, and so much more!

Metal clay is an air-dry product that needs to be fired at high temperatures to transform from dried "clay" to metal. During the firing process, the clay sinters; after the binder has burned away, the metal coalesces to form a solid mass.

Metal clay starts to shrink during the drying process and shrinks even more during the firing process. Each brand has its own shrinkage factor, and within each brand there is a range. For Art Clay Silver, the range is 8%–12%, with the variance dependent upon the dimension and thickness of the material pre-firing.

Once fired, the clay can be worked like metal, because—it is! You can form, shape, polish, solder, and more. The beauty of metal clay, though, is all the "metal" work can be done during the "clay" phase, so there is little more than polishing needed once your designs are fired. Those more familiar working with metal might prefer refining and finishing post-firing.

The projects in this book are made using all forms of fine-silver metal clay: lump, paste, syringe, and paper.

> **Lump form**—the go-to for the main structure of your design
>
> **Paste**—a spreadable clay used for assembling, adding embellishments, and more
>
> **Syringe**—similar to paste but thin enough it can be extruded through a fine-tip nozzle of a syringe yet hold dimension; great for drawing or writing in metal clay
>
> **Sheet/paper**—a unique formula of metal clay that does not dry out and has a suede-like feel; can be cut with scissors, paper-punched, folded like origami, and so much more

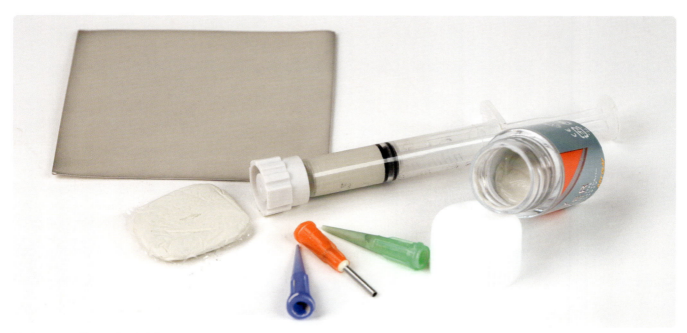

Most common forms of metal clay

16 | PROJECTS & TECHNIQUES FOR METAL CLAY JEWELRY

Basic assembly of tools and materials for setting up to work with clay

BASIC SETUP

Before I begin working with metal clay, I set up my workstation with the following tools:

- Work surface: glass base and, often, a non-stick platform
- Non-stick sheets/cards
- Paintbrush
- Water dish with sponge
- Acrylic roller
- Awl / clay pick
- Silicone-tipped tool
- Tweezers
- Gauges/cards
- Fine-mist spray bottle with distilled water
- Non-stick lubricant / release agent

Work Surface

When deciding what to use as your base for clay work, consider using a smooth work surface when rolling out your clay. My favorite is a piece of (safety) glass or an acrylic sheet, since they do not add any unwanted texture. Depending on the project, I also employ a platform with a non-stick sheet.

Once the clay is rolled to the correct thickness, I transfer it to a small non-stick sheet. On this sheet, I can cut out the clay, move it around more easily to see it from all vantage points, and remove it altogether from the main work surface, so I'm free to do more clay work while the work-in-progress pieces are drying.

Artist-Quality Paintbrush

Paintbrushes are wonderful for smoothing the clay, adding just the right amount of water when needed, applying paste-type clay, and so much more. Using a quality brush ensures the best experience; having a few different shapes and sizes of brushes is also advisable.

Spray Bottle with Water, a Dish with Water, and Sponge

Having water nearby is a convenience. A spray bottle helps apply just the right amount of water when rehydrating clay. A small dish of water is great for dipping

TOOLS AND MATERIALS | 17

your paintbrush into. A sponge helps remove excess water and clay paste from the paintbrush.

Acrylic Roller
Any type of roller will work to flatten clay, but an acrylic roller offers a smooth surface and doesn't impart unwanted texture.

Fine-Tipped Awl or Needle Tool
A fine-tipped tool can be used to cut through the clay, pick up excess clay, remove fine debris, and more. Having a fine, sharp, strong tip is key for creating a clean edge and having little drag when used on the clay.

Silicone/Rubber-Tipped Tool
This tool is great for smoothing, contouring, cleaning edges, removing debris, and anything that your finger wants to do but shouldn't. (Fingers leave fingerprints and dents and can misshape the surface.)

   I love the silicone-tipped tools and the availability of so many different shapes and firmness. I have many on hand but keep just a few at my side for daily use. I prefer something with a stiffness that has a little give, a fine point but rounded edge.

Release Agent
Olive oil or silicone-based products work well with metal clay and help prevent the clay from sticking to your tools, work surface, and hands. There are many products on the market manufactured for this purpose, but you can use olive oil from your kitchen.

   A light coating is usually all you need. Too much and your clay will slide around or wind up in puddles on the surface—not something you need or want to have happen. While excessive olive oil / release products don't seem to hurt or change the clay, to me it changes the texture of the clay over time, so I use it as sparingly as possible.

   To use: apply a few spritzes or swipes to your hands, then smooth over your tools and work surface; spritz your textures before using them so the clay doesn't wind up *in* the texture. There is nothing fun about digging clay out of a texture mat.

   When working with clay, if you find it sticks too much, it might be too wet.

   When this happens, I place the clay into a piece of plastic wrap and condition it a bit by kneading until the surface is silky smooth and the clay is no longer sticking to the wrapping.

Examples of a few gauges available: playing cards, rolling frames, gauges, plastic slats

18 | PROJECTS & TECHNIQUES FOR METAL CLAY JEWELRY

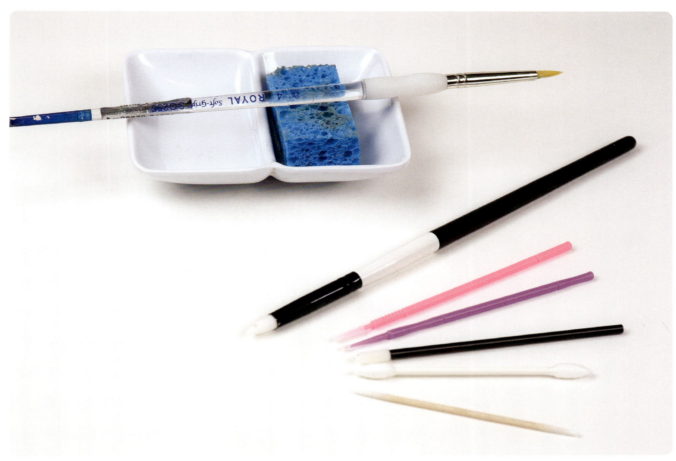

Examples of tools used to refine the clay while still wet: water, sponge, paintbrush, silicone-tipped tool, and makeup applicators

THICKNESS GUIDES/GAUGES

Gauges, or cards, are used to control the thickness of the clay as it is rolled flat. In metal clay, we often refer to the thickness in how many "cards thick." This term came about since playing cards were used when the clay was new to the market. It was an accessible tool and made it easy to communicate how a design was made, and so anyone could remake or test the same example regardless of location.

Today, you can still use playing cards or any of the tools made that use the same measuring dimension of "cards thick," as well as millimeters.

TOOLS FOR REFINING THE SURFACE: WET CLAY

When shaping the clay, whether cutting using metal cutters or a fine-tipped tool, the edges need cleaning up. Water helps smooth cut edges as well as refine any imperfections. Apply water with an artist's-quality paintbrush, and you can remove nearly all imperfections in wet clay before you set it aside to dry. Silicone-tipped tools are also great for cleaning up and moving the clay while it is still wet. I always keep a variety of makeup applicators on hand, since they make it easier to get into smaller areas.

NOTE: It is best to clean up the clay at each stage, so you minimize waste and save time as your design progresses.

TOOLS AND MATERIALS | 19

A sample of textures used throughout this book: rubber stamps, metal stamps, laser-cut paper, silicone texture mats, metal texture plates

TEXTURE TOOLS

One of the qualities I love most about metal clay is its ability to take on texture. The shrinkage that occurs during firing only amplifies any texture you apply. The tools you can use to apply texture are limitless.

CUTTING TOOLS

My favorite tools for cutting clay are a fine-pointed awl and manufactured templates or templates I create myself. Shaped cutters work well and can be found through different disciplines—cooking, hobby stores, etc.

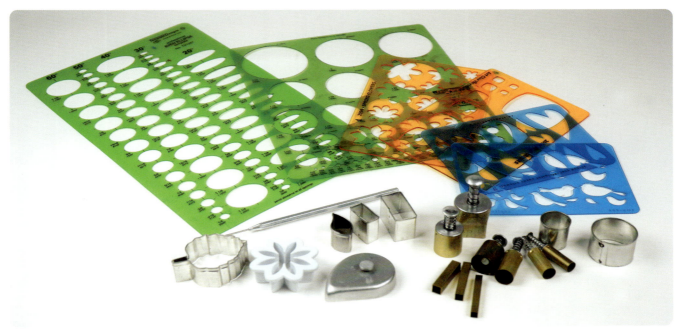

Sampling of tools you can use to cut metal clay: templates and a fine-tipped awl, cookie cutters, fondant cutter, brass tubing, and clay cutters

TOOLS FOR FORMING WET CLAY

After you cut the clay, it can be dried flat. To add dimension during the wet-clay stage, you can dry the clay over a form. You can use any surface except aluminum, since aluminum can cause an adverse reaction and hinder the finished design during the firing process.

Keep in mind that, when you fire the clay, gravity will take over and the clay will become flat. To retain the desired curves and dimension, use heat-safe materials. (See "Firing the Clay," page 50.)

Wet clay can be shaped over forms. Forming tool examples include wooden dapping blocks, plastic forming devices, silicone molds, paint palettes, and dapped brass discs.

TOOLS AND MATERIALS | 21

Refining tools I prefer include salon boards, micron-graded polishing papers, small abrasive sticks, and jeweler's files.

TOOLS FOR REFINING THE SURFACE: DRY CLAY

Once the clay is dry, you can further refine the surface by using a variety of abrasives. A salon board in medium to fine grit will do the heavy lifting. Follow with polishing papers (a personal favorite)—they are flexible pieces of micron-graded paper available in a range of grits. Get into openings or hard-to-reach places with jeweler's files (dedicated to metal clay) or abrasive sanding sticks.

FIRING
Butane Torch

For most metal clays, it is recommended to fire by using a kiln to reach proper sintering temperature and hold time. It is, however, possible to achieve the same results by using a butane torch, with just a few caveats. I prefer to use a handheld butane torch that is well made and rated to reach above 2,000°F. I recommend using only filtered butane fuel for the sake and longevity of your torch.

Fire on a heatproof surface, then on top of a fire brick or kiln shelf / solderite board. Always have on hand a timer, fire extinguisher / fire blanket, heatproof gloves, long tweezers, and water. (For more on firing with a torch, see "Firing the Clay," page 50.)

A metal clay design up to 25 grams in size can be fired using a butane torch.

22 | PROJECTS & TECHNIQUES FOR METAL CLAY JEWELRY

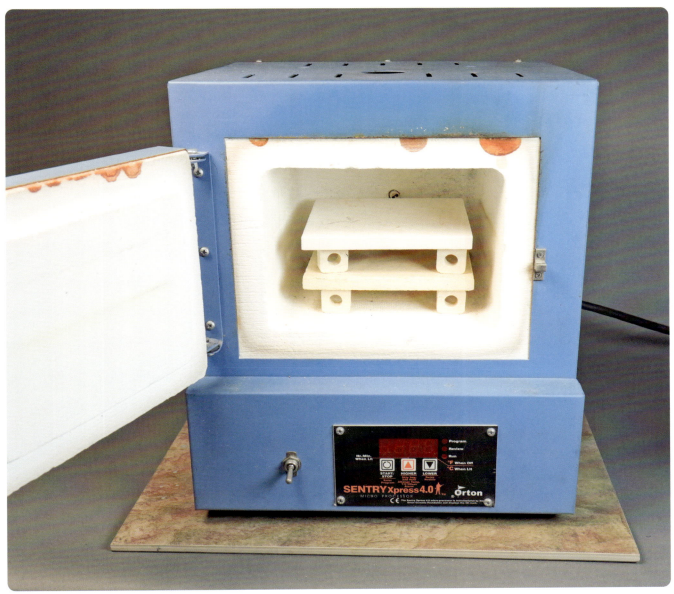

Most any type of kiln will work for firing metal clay. A tabletop-size kiln that can reach 1,650°F is all you need for successfully firing a design.

Kiln

I prefer to work with a tabletop kiln with a controller built in. It makes it possible to successfully fire without having to watch the kiln for an entire cycle. My kiln is placed on a heatproof surface, and I always ensure there is nothing in the immediate area that could be affected by the heat the kiln throws off. Please note: the heat is minimal, but it is always better to be safe and proactive in preventing any unwanted accidents. Place finished pieces onto a kiln shelf, not the kiln floor. When needed for housing more designs than one kiln shelf can fit, stack shelves, using kiln furniture. (For more on firing with a kiln, see "Firing the Clay," page 50.)

TOOLS AND MATERIALS | 23

It is important to be prepared for any accidents that can occur in your studio.

SAFETY EQUIPMENT

I always keep on hand a particulate mask for use when handling materials like vermiculite. It can also be used when working / sanding dry clay if you have any sensitivities. Be prepared when firing with a torch, just in case. Keep a fire extinguisher, fire blanket, bowl of water, tweezers, and fireproof gloves handy.

POLISHING THE SURFACE

Once the metal has been fired and cooled, it's time to polish and bring up that shine. To start, you can use a brass brush to burnish the surface. Follow that with a metal or agate burnisher. You can further polish by using a tumbler and mixed stainless-steel shot or pin finisher. You can also do all the finish work using a motorized tool. (For more on polishing, see "Finishing," page 53.)

Use a series of tools to polish the clay to achieve the highest shine your design calls for.

24 | PROJECTS & TECHNIQUES FOR METAL CLAY JEWELRY

CHAPTER 2
Techniques

Metal clay can be rolled, flattened, shaped, layered, stamped, carved (when dry), and so much more. Metal clay is considerably easy to work with in any studio. The tools you need are minimal (although there are many more you may want!), you need little space to work, and you can be creative in how you fire your finished designs.

Metal clay has its nuances, and it doesn't always naturally do what you need or want it to do. Once you have a handle on techniques and the clay's temperament, working with the materials is a dream.

There are a variety of metal clays on the market and different manufacturers. The following information references fine-silver metal clay.

Starter Tips

- Clay is packaged to prevent moisture loss—it does have a shelf life—this is based on the possibility of moisture loss and the change in the pliability of the clay over time.
- Once the package is opened, covering clay with plastic cling wrap or storing under a glass spritzed with water (like a humidifier) willhelp retain moisture and working condition.
- While the clay is in the wet stage, spritz the surface with a bit of distilled water when the clay appears to be drying/cracking; allow the water to absorb before working with it.
- Applying a release agent to your hands, work surface, and tools prior to working with the clay will help prevent the clay from sticking.
- Metal clay is an air-dry product and should be handled with care so it doesn't dry out prematurely. To prevent drying, cover the clay with or store in plastic wrap.
- Drying time will vary based on conditions in the room and your environment.
- Clay must be dry before firing, or the remaining moisture will escape and alter the surface of your design during the firing process.

- You can store clay (even in unopened packaging) in an airtight container with a damp paper towel or sponge tucked inside. Use distilled water for this process, to prevent too much mold from forming during storage.
- Any mold formed on or around the clay during storage has not been found to cause any problems with the clay, so in my experience, it is still safe to use.
- Aluminum tools can be used when working with metal clay, but don't allow metal clay to dry on an aluminum form. DO NOT incorporate any metal clay particles that may have dried on an aluminum tool into your clay or clay paste. There is a chance of an adverse chemical reaction between metal clay and aluminum, which will not yield desired results.
- Use a soft brush to remove all clay dust before firing, or the dust could fire in place.
- There is a misconception that the clay has a white film or residue on the surface after firing. There is no residue but rather a bumpy surface that cannot reflect light—knock down the bumps with burnishing and light will reflect and the metal shine!

Fresh Out of the Package

ROLLING OUT A SHEET OF CLAY AND ADDING TEXTURE

Create an even thickness of clay by rolling across gauges, then add texture for interest.

All projects in this book with rolling involved will indicate how many "cards" or millimeters to roll to, so you know how thick the piece should be to achieve the desired result, as well as so the design can hold up to wear and tear. You can adjust the recommendation as you gain experience and an understanding of how your design will be worn. Bracelets should always be thicker (4 or 3 cards thick), while a charm could be as thin as 2 cards thick.

Determine the thickness you need for the project you are working on, then add at least "1-card" thickness if you'll be adding texture. This addition will allow the clay to be rolled thinner when you add the texture. If using a deep-textured mat or tool, start with a sheet of clay that is 2 cards thicker than your final thickness.

Prepare your work surface, hands, rollers, and texture.

NOTE: Follow manufacturers' recommendations so you're sure your texturing tool is prepared properly before use. Some products require time in between application and use, and spending time digging clay out of a texture is not fun!

Cards Thick—Millimeters

- ½-card thick, 0.005"/0.125 mm
- 1-card thick, 0.01"/0.25 mm
- 2-cards thick, 0.02"/0.50 mm
- 3 cards thick, 0.03"/0.75 mm
- 4 cards thick, 0.04"/1 mm
- 6 cards thick, 0.06"/1.5 mm
- 8-cards thick, 0.08"/2 mm

Place a lump of metal clay between playing cards, plastic slats, or inside a frame.

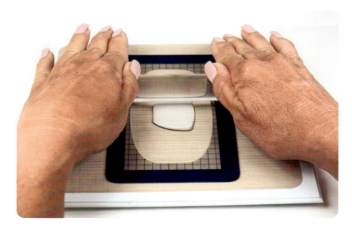

Roll across the clay, using an acrylic roller. Roll until the clay is to the thickness of the gauges you're using.

TIP: As needed, move the clay in a way that stretches it to suit the design you're working toward (keep it long and thin, flip it a quarter turn midway through to create a square dimension, etc.).

Place the thinner gauges along each edge of a textured sheet. Place the clay onto the textured sheet between the guides. Using the acrylic roller, firmly roll across the surface of the clay.

Once you think you have achieved your desired impression, lift the clay to see if the impression is as you intended. If not, restart by compressing the clay back into a lump form.

Move the textured clay to a non-stick sheet.

CUTTING OUT WET CLAY
Using the textured sheet, cut out a shape.

Place the appropriate template or cutter onto the clay, positioned so you are capturing the texture or the area of the smooth sheet of your choice. If using a template, place the tip of an awl along the inside edge, then cut out the shape. If you use a cutter, press firmly through the clay.

If your finished design will need a hole for adding your component after firing, place a pilot hole in the fresh clay state. The hole can be enlarged using a jeweler's file, in the dry state. Do not put this hole too close to the edge; when the clay is fired, the distance between the hole and the edge will shrink and make it vulnerable to wear.

ROLLING A ROPE OF CLAY

Using a clean, dry cloth, clean your work surface. Having clean, untreated surfaces is key to this technique. Use a piece of smooth acrylic as a rolling tool. You will want to work as quickly as possible as you are exposing more clay to the air and it will dry much more quickly.

Pinch off 5–10 grams of clay from the package. Roll the clay into a cylindrical shape to help get the process started.

To dry the clay flat, put the non-stick sheet aside so the clay can dry. To form or dome clay, carefully transfer a cut piece of clay to a mold or form, either face down or up depending on the design effect you are going for. Gently press into place. Allow to dry.

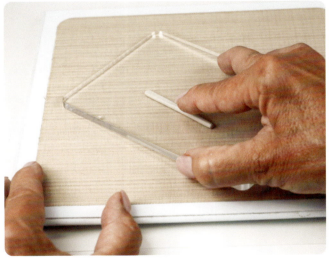

Place the acrylic sheet or "snake roller" on top of the cylinder of clay. Move the acrylic sheet forward and back, rolling the clay so it thins and grows in length. Continue to move quickly, putting downward pressure on the acrylic sheet, so the clay grows in length but does not get flattened. Roll to the thickness you need for your project.

TECHNIQUES | 29

OPTION:
Taper one end of a rope.

I love being able to create a tapered round rope and often do this to form a spiral, which can then be made into a charm or element you add to a design.

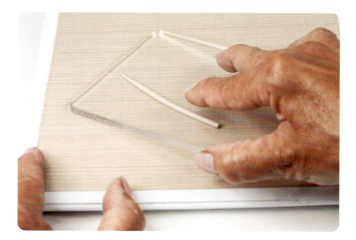

Create a rope of clay. As the rope gets longer, put more pressure on one end of the acrylic rectangle, creating a thinner end on one side of the rope. Create a rope as long as you need for your design.

Using a paintbrush, lightly wet the tapered end of the rope.

Begin to nudge the end into an inward curve. Don't press so hard that the clay cleaves, but press hard enough that the clay knows you're in charge.

Continue to work the curve into a spiral, working your way down the length of the rope.

OPTION:
Create a coil from a rope of clay.

I like to make a few coils before starting any project, so I can create jumprings and bails that match my design. I make a variety of coils in different thicknesses and sizes. Control the thickness by the size of rope you roll out; control the size by the cylinder you wrap the rope around. I use straws or similar tools for this process—choose something that has a little bit of give so it's easier to slide the coil off as it begins to dry.

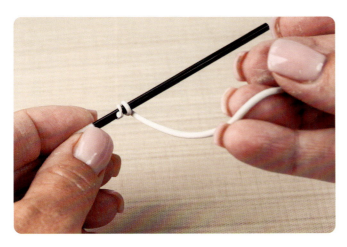

After rolling into a rope, anchor one end of the rope to the end of the cylinder you've chosen to wrap the coil around.

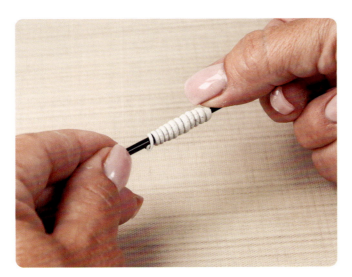

Turn the cylinder, winding the clay around into a coil. Anchor the other end of the rope to the cylinder so the coil does not unfurl.

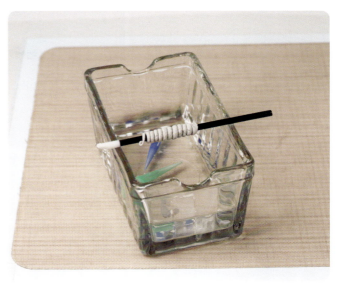

Rest the cylindrical tool across two surfaces while the clay dries—this will help maintain the rounded profile of the rope.

Allow the clay to dry for a little bit, until firm. Carefully, so you don't crush the coil, slip the coil off the cylinder and onto your work surface. Allow to dry fully.

TECHNIQUES | 31

To create rings, using a sharp blade, cut the coil between each wrapped section.

To create jumprings, trim the ends so they meet up squarely.

To create a loop or bail for adding to a pendant or charm, trim the ends of the ring above center or less, so you leave a curve with the dimension you need for the design.

Add a bail to create a pendant or charm

Allow both the bail and your design to dry fully. File the ends of the bail so they match the contour of the design you're adding it to.

Check the fit.

Apply a bit of water to each piece where they will be joined, and allow the water to absorb.

Dip the ends of the bail into metal clay paste.

Add the bail to the prepared area of your design. Allow the fresh clay paste to dry fully before moving the design.

Once dry, check for any gaps in the joint. If you see any, add a little water, then more clay, and allow to dry again. Once the joint is sure, you can refine the area with sanding materials. (For more on sanding, see "Refining Dried Metal Clay," page 36.)

JOINING WET CLAY TO WET CLAY

There are two important factors for joining wet clay to wet clay—water and pressure. This is also a technique that can be tricky, since you're usually trying not to mar the surface but need to apply pressure and handle the clay while it's wet.

Press the top or second layer of clay to the wet area of clay to create a join. Apply pressure either with a tool or a finger treated with a release agent. Apply additional water, if necessary.

TIP: A silicone tool or bit of release agent will help prevent tools or your finger (or both) from sticking to the wet clay when applying pressure.

Create the base of your design. Using a paintbrush, apply water to the areas you want to join.

Using a paintbrush, clean up the join and ensure that the seam is sealed.

Allow the clay to dry. Using slip or paste, fill in any areas that are not smooth and sealed. Allow to dry again. Once dried completely, refine the area as needed. (For more on finishing dried clay, see "Refining Dried Metal Clay," page 36.)

Drying Before Its Time

REFRESHING METAL CLAY

As metal clay is worked into designs, inevitably there are pieces of clay left over. Gather these pieces as you go, wrapping them into a piece of cling wrap. When you're ready to work with this portion of clay, you might notice it is not as workable as it was when you first opened the clay package. That is normal and an inherent quality in the clay. With a little bit of water and patience, you can bring it back to its working state.

NOTE: These instructions apply to most metal clay. Please check the manufacturer's instructions, since different brands can react differently or need alternative treatment.

Continue to fold or knead the clay in this manner. It might be a little challenging at the start, with the clay sliding around if you applied too much water. Just keep going. Clay does not like to absorb water, so it takes some time and patience.

While the clay is in plastic wrap, add a few spritzes of distilled water or a suitable clay-rehydrating formula.

As you make progress, you will see the clay return to "normal" and have a silky appearance. Once you've reached this state and the clay is rehydrated, pinch a piece of clay from the lump. It should feel as fresh as it did when you first opened the clay pack, and you shouldn't have any clay sticking to your fingers.

Fold the clay in half, onto itself.

Working with (Intentionally) Dried Clay

DRYING METAL CLAY

Metal clay is an air-dry material. You can leave the clay open on any work surface and it will dry fully, in time—humidity and room temperature are a factor in this process, so timing will vary from place to place and during different times of year.

When working on a design, you may want to expedite the drying so you can work on your pieces more quickly. There are a few tools you can use for this purpose.
- Candle / mug-warming plate
- Griddle

REFINING DRIED METAL CLAY

It is advisable to refine or finish the surface of dried metal clay prior to firing. This will ensure that your piece comes out of the kiln with the best possible finish and requires minimal work to polish it.

Refining Tips

Before you begin refining metal clay, clean your work surface so when you capture your "sanding dust," it doesn't contain anything else but metal clay and can be repurposed into paste or slip.

Drying Tips

When expediting drying, the water will evaporate more quickly than the clay prefers, and you may find the surface warping. To help combat this, flip the design over periodically and allow gravity to help retain your preferred dimension.

If the clay dries in a shape or form you do not desire, you can apply a mist of water or even pat water onto the surface of dried clay, using a paintbrush. Allow the water to absorb, and the clay will soften and take the shape of the form it's resting on. You may need to apply light pressure—if so, do not press so firmly that you alter the design or texture applied to the surface.

Allow the clay to dry fully before proceeding to the next steps in your project.

If you try to refine the surface of clay before it's fully dry, you will feel a bit of a drag on the sanding tools or see a darker color of clay below the surface. You should stop at this discovery and allow the clay to dry further.

If you fire the clay and there is still moisture present, the water will need to escape and will likely cause pocks in the surface of the clay.

The clay is at its most fragile and vulnerable state when dry, so support the piece as best as you can—hold against your finger and only have a small amount of the design above your finger as you sand.

Refining can be done with various tools and sanding materials. Always work from the lowest (coarsest) grit to the highest.

Do not remove more material than is necessary—you do not want your metal clay design to become too thin, or to remove too much of the applied texture or design elements.

When you're ready to fire a design, use a soft brush to remove any remaining "clay dust," since it could otherwise fire in place.

Collect particles of dried clay and save them in a small container. Label the container so you can identify the type of clay in the container.

Add distilled water to the container of dried "clay dust" to form your own metal clay paste. Stir well so you create a smooth paste.

TECHNIQUES | 37

Example of joining dry clay to dry clay

JOINING DRY CLAY TO DRY CLAY

Complex designs can be created by joining dried, refined clay to dried refined clay. Create the components of your design, allow them to dry thoroughly, then refine to near perfection. The reason for all the prep is so that the next steps are all you have to address rather than having to refine the whole design. This not only helps make the process more efficient but also reduces the risk of breakage or separating the pieces at the new joint.

Apply water to each part of the design being joined together. The water wakes the dry clay up and makes it more willing to receive what's next.

On one layer of your design, apply a thick layer of paste-type clay, using a paintbrush or silicone/rubber-tipped tool.

Apply a thick layer of slip or paste-type clay to the second layer. Press the two layers together. Using the paintbrush, apply a bit of water and neaten up any slip that has "oozed" out between the joint.

NOTE: *You want the slip to be thick in this area as well as have excess ooze out; however, it does not need to be messy. Excess paste-type clay will shrink inward, so it will naturally be reduced in scale, but extra excess will need to be cleaned up, so the seam is invisible. It's a balancing act.*

Allow the clay to dry; fill in any areas that are not smooth and sealed. Allow to dry again.

Once dried completely, refine the area as needed. (For more on finishing a design, see "Refining Dried Metal Clay," page 36.)

Coloring Outside the (Clay) Box

USING THE SYRINGE-TYPE CLAY TO DECORATE AND EMBELLISH A DESIGN

Syringe type clay can be used for embellishing or even as structure in a design (see "Masked Texture Pendant," page 92); you can use it like you would jewelry wire. Syringe-type clay is a different formula from the other types of clay, so ensure that you use a thicker extrusion of syringe-type clay if used for any structural elements.

Syringe Tips

Keep the tip of your syringe submerged in water while creating a design; otherwise the clay in the tip will dry out and you will need to replace the tip with a new one.

When you're done using the syringe, remove the active syringe tip and replace it with the original cap.

Store the syringe with a bit of water inside a sealed container, to prolong the longevity of the clay inside.

You can use syringe-type clay like you would jewelry wire. It can be used to create loops, decorations, bails, etc. However, I prefer to use lump clay for many of these elements, since it is stronger and will hold up better to wear and tear.

I will often extrude a "line" of syringe and hold it aloft until I know I risk it drooping. I will then slowly lay it down onto my design. This action gives me greater control over how it is added to the design. And this takes practice.

Finely extruded syringe-type clay should be connected to the surface of the item you're adding it to. If left unattached, the clay will still fire but will be fragile and susceptible to catching on something or breaking off. To ensure the layers are connected, use a paintbrush and water to flood the area where you've applied the syringe-type clay along with the applied syringe-type clay, then gently press the two together. Work carefully so you retain the dimension of the syringed clay.

Place the appropriate syringe tip on the end of the syringe.

Create a piece and refine it until it is perfect and ready for firing. Using a paintbrush, wet the surface to be decorated.

Depress the plunger slowly to release a little bit of clay, as well as any trapped air.

Extrude the clay onto the design.

Using the paintbrush, wet the surface again along with the extruded syringe-type clay, working carefully so you don't compress the surface of the extruded clay.

Gently press on the extruded syringe-type clay to secure the two surfaces together. Make any minor adjustments you feel are needed. Let the clay dry.

Once dry, check to make sure the extruded clay has adhered to the surface of the design. If there are any gaps, fill in the spaces by using the syringe- or paste-type clay. Let dry.

TECHNIQUES | 41

CREATING FINE SILVER GRANULES FROM PAPER-TYPE CLAY

Materials you need:
- • Paper-type clay
- • Hole punch
- • Firebrick
- • Bowl of water
- • Small container
- • Safety equipment (see page 24)

Using the hole punch, punch holes in the sheet-type clay.

You will see a red glow, which is usually when the granule has formed, and you can move on to the next. Repeat working on all the circles you punched out. If you find any did not fully form, you can reheat as needed.

Place the circles of clay you cut out onto the firebrick. Light a torch; so the flame does not blow the clay circles away, carefully heat the circles until they draw up and form a ball or granule.

Allow the granules to cool, then roll them into a water bath. I do this to help rinse the granules and free them from any firebrick debris that might stick to them.

Place the fine-silver granules into a container and keep them handy to add to a design (see "Layered Bracelet Link," page 78).

Taking Matters into Your Own Hands

CREATING A TWO-PART SILICONE MOLD AND METAL CLAY MOLDED DESIGN

There are premade molds available on the market, but you can also make your own! Choose nearly any object to cast into silicone, then use the finished mold to create a finished version in metal clay.

Follow the manufacturer's instructions when creating your mold. The following is a general guideline that works with most compounds. When working with any two-part formula, the proper chemical reaction occurs when you work with equal portions of each part. A scale is the best tool for measuring out each part.

Begin to blend the two parts together.

From part A, scoop out a little more than half of what you need to create a mold for your chosen item. Measure this portion and set it aside. Clean off your hands or the tool you used for scooping, then repeat for part B.

Working quickly, blend until the compound is one uniform color.

Once the compound is completely blended, form the mass into a shape suitable for the object you're molding. Flatten slightly.

TECHNIQUES | 43

Create a Component from a Mold

Press the item to be molded into the molding compound, so the entire shape is captured and the item is level. Allow the item and compound to rest until the compound is cured. Curing time varies depending on the brand you're using.

Pinch off enough clay to fill the mold. Form the clay into the rough shape of the mold.

TIP: You'll know when the compound is cured when you can press your fingernail into the side of the compound and your nail doesn't leave a mark.

Press the clay into the mold so it fills the space created by your object and sits level.

Once it's cured, remove the item from the mold.

OPTIONAL: Press a texture onto the backside of the clay, so both the front and the back will hold details.

Set aside until the clay is dry. Drying time will vary based on conditions in the room and your environment.

44 | PROJECTS & TECHNIQUES FOR METAL CLAY JEWELRY

TIP: You may find the clay takes longer to dry inside the mold. To expedite, wait about thirty minutes, carefully release the clay from the mold, and allow to dry fully.

Allow the design to dry fully, then refine with sanding materials to prepare for firing. (For more on sanding, see "Refining Dried Metal Clay," page 36.)

TECHNIQUES | 45

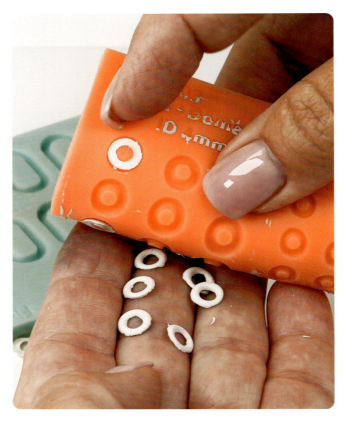

CREATING EMBELLISHMENTS FROM MANUFACTURED MOLDS

Create embellishments from molds and use as elements or decorations for a design. The molds shown here are used in projects within this book. They are manufactured by Cool Tools USA, but there are others on the market that work similarly.

While applying downward pressure, drag the scraper across the surface of the mold. This action will force clay into the recesses. *NOTE: The best results I have found come when you fill the recess in one pass. You can go back in and refill any gaps there might be, but you might have additional cleanup after the elements are dry.*

Drag the tool across the surface again, to remove excess clay and ensure a smooth "bottom" for the elements. This will help alleviate some cleanup after the elements have dried.

Place a bit of clay at the top of the area you are working on creating elements from. Place a very fine scraper (the tool shown is from the clay industry) and angle it.

46 | PROJECTS & TECHNIQUES FOR METAL CLAY JEWELRY

CREATE YOUR OWN TEXTURE PLATE

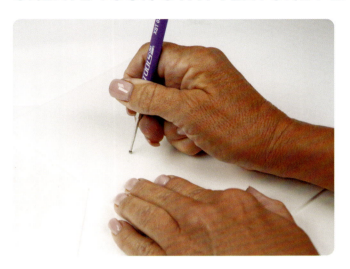 

When working with metal clay, texture is the name of the game for me. I use a lot of textures found around my home and yard, through my travels, and in stamps and mats made by a variety of manufacturers and artists.

I also like to make my own, using tools I have in my studio. Using different tools like ball-tip stylus, I create simple line drawings. These textures translate well in clay. The texture of these plates also plays a part in the design, so keep that in mind if you choose to use the foam sheets for your own texture mats.

TECHNIQUES | 47

ATTACHING FINE SILVER FINDINGS

Depending on the clay, you can fire in place fine and sterling silver findings, wire, and more. The following steps are for fine-silver clay and a two-part fine-silver brooch finding.

Prepare your design until it's as perfect as you can get it. Wet the area in which you will be placing the finding, and allow the water to absorb. Meanwhile, apply a bit of clay to the base of one-half of the finding.

Press the finding to the prepared area. Use a silicone-tipped tool to blend the fresh clay to the dried clay.

Repeat, placing the other half of the finding opposite the first half.

Check to make sure the findings are positioned directly across from each other, so the pin will line up straight once the brooch is fired and so they are placed the right distance from each other to accommodate the length of the pin.

TIP: If placing the finding so it lines up horizontally, it's good to have the finding placed above the center of the brooch, so it doesn't flop forward when you wear it.

Refine the entire surface of the brooch prior to firing, and remove any remaining particles from the surface of the brooch before firing it. (For more information, see "Refining Dried Metal Clay," page 36.)

48 | PROJECTS & TECHNIQUES FOR METAL CLAY JEWELRY

Attaching the Pin to the Pin Finding

Once the design is fired and polished, check the length of the pin against the space between the two halves of the pin finding. If the pin extends past the end of the brooch, use flush-cut pliers to trim to the appropriate length. Make sure you don't cut it too short—the point of the pin should extend just past the catch of the pin finding, but not past the edge of the brooch.

Use jeweler's files and sanding materials, working from the lowest to the highest grit, to resharpen the end of the pin.

Position the circle end of the pin into the hinge half of the pin finding, so the knobs on the inside of the finding fit into the open circle. Using chain-nose pliers, close the pin finding to secure the pin.

Ensure that the catch is open enough to accommodate the pin, but not so much the pin doesn't stay in place when worn.

FIRING THE CLAY

Metal clay must be fired to a temperature of at least 1,110°F. Use a kiln to fire metal clay for optimum results—a butane torch can be used for pieces smaller than 25 grams.

To ensure the greatest success, follow the manufacturer's directions for the brand of metal clay you're using.

Be sure to fire safely and with a fire extinguisher, water, tweezers, and fire-safe gloves on hand.

Firing a Flat Design in a Kiln

For designs that are flat, you can place them directly onto a kiln shelf—NOT the kiln floor.

Firing a Domed or Shaped Design in a Kiln

For designs that have dimension or depth, you want to support them in the firing process. The metal gets hot in the kiln; gravity will take over without the support, and your piece can wind up flat or misshapen.

Vermiculite (a soil additive found at local nurseries) is a great material for supporting clay at high temperatures.

When using vermiculite, always wear a dust mask.

- Put vermiculite onto the kiln shelf or into a kiln-safe container.
- Place the domed or shaped components on top of the vermiculite and nestle the piece(s) into place.
- Fire the kiln following the clay manufacturer's recommended temperature and time.
- Let the components cool to room temperature, then finish accordingly.

Firing with a Butane Torch

Fine silver metal clay can be fired to the proper temperature and held for a suitable amount of time to reach sintering, using a butane torch.

- Be sure to work in a well-ventilated area and on a heatproof surface.
- Place a fire block onto the heatproof surface.
- Following the instructions for your butane torch, fill the chamber with butane fuel. Set your timer for 2½ minutes.
- For safety purposes, have a pair of long-handled tweezers and a bowl of cold water near where you are working. Put on your safety glasses.

- *TIP: Dim the lights in the work area, if possible, so you can see the color of the piece while firing.*
- Place the metal clay design onto the fire block. Press the safety on the torch, ignite the torch, then press the switch to keep the flame lit. (This will enable you to work without having to hold the trigger of the torch the whole time.)
- Begin to heat the design, working the flame around in a circular pattern. Soon, you will see smoke, then a small flame. That is the indicator that the binder is burning off—if you look closely, you will also notice that the piece has shrunk.
- The piece will likely curl as it shrinks further. It will eventually flatten back out.
- Continue to heat the piece until it reaches a peachy-salmon color.
- Once the piece reaches the peachy-salmon color, hit the timer and begin the 2½-minute countdown.
- Continue to heat the piece, maintaining the color, working the flame over the entire surface in a circular pattern. This will help ensure that the piece is heated properly.

TECHNIQUES | 51

- *TIP: If the design begins to appear shiny (it is getting too hot and will soon melt!), don't stop the torch but, rather, pull the torch back from the piece so the flame isn't too close. Continue to heat the piece and maintain the peachy-salmon color.*
- Once you have fired the piece for 2½ minutes, you can turn off the torch and set it aside. Let the piece cool to room temperature.

- OPTIONAL: Move the piece from the brick to a bowl of water to ensure it is fully cooled.
- Finish accordingly.

Finishing

Once fired, metal clay is metal. Therefore, it can be worked like metal, using metalworking tools. The surface of fired metal clay will appear white once cooled; this is quickly remedied by changing the topography of the silver. There are a variety of ways this can be achieved. Included are the ones I used most.

Rotary tumbler barrels filled with media for tumbling. (Left) mixed stainless-steel shot; (right) silicon carbide, Hone & Highlight mini media.

Polishing with a Tumbler

Tumble polishing with mixed stainless-steel shot will bring a brass-brushed design to a high-shine polish. Tumble polishing a brass-brushed design with a silicon carbide medium will further work the design, burnishing the fine details, and leave you with a satiny-matte finish.

Tumble polishing is a method I use often, since it frees up my time and my hands.

Follow the manufacturer's instructions for your tumbler and use the appropriate amount of burnishing solution.

- Place your items into a barrel filled with your chosen media.
- Fill to just above the surface of the contents with burnishing solution.
- Replace the lid and secure.
- Let the tumbler run for twenty minutes, then check progress.
- If needed, run the tumbler longer until the desired finish is achieved.
- Dump the stainless-steel shot and components into a sieve over a bucket.
- Remove the jewelry components and rinse them with soap and water.
- Let dry.
- Return the shot to the tumbler barrel for storage, or leave it in the sieve undisturbed until it is dry, then place in a zip-top bag.
- Dispose the water in the bucket as you would other wash water.

Brass Brushing

- A soft brass brush will work quickly to burnish the surface of fired metal clay and will leave a satiny finish.
- A rubber block is a great way to lift the piece off the work surface, as well as offering a bit of a grip to help keep the piece in place while you brush.
- A lubricant, such as dish soap, will help the brush glide more easily and prevent transferring brass to the surface of the silver.
- Stabilize the fired design. Apply a small dab of lubricant. Brush across the entire surface until you achieve a silvery-satin finish.
- Further enhance the shine of the silver by going over the surface with an agate or steel burnisher.

TECHNIQUES | 53

For my rotary tumbler, I use 2 pounds of mixed shot and can place about twenty charms or five to seven larger pieces in at a time (maybe more!). I tumble for about twenty minutes with great results. For pieces with finer detail, I use the silicon carbide media first, since it gets into the grooves missed by the brass brush. Depending on the design, I will then tumble in mixed stainless-steel shot.

After adding a patina (see "Adding a Patina with Liver of Sulfur Gel," page 55), I tumble all pieces in the mini silicon carbide as it burnishes the surface, leaving the patina right where I want it. I only run the tumbler for a quick ten minutes, checking progress after five minutes to be sure I don't remove too much patina. To burnish the surface to a higher polish, rinse the pieces after tumbling with the silicon carbide, then place into the pin finisher for five minutes.

Polishing with a Pin Finisher

You can place your fired metal clay pieces (after cooling) right from the kiln into a pin finisher. Let the finisher do its work for about fifteen minutes, then choose to tumble in mixed stainless-steel shot for a higher polish, go right to patina, or place into a finished design.

- With the pins already inside, add your fired pieces (only put in a few at a time until you know how many is too many).
- Add your preferred solution to the container, following manufacturer's instructions for how much fluid to use.
- Turn the machine on, medium speed and ten minutes to start.
- At the end of the time set, assess progress. Add more time and consider greater speed if needed.
- Once the pieces have been finished to your liking, remove them from the container, being careful to leave the pins behind.
- Wash the pieces in soap and water.
- Keep a magnet nearby to pick up any stray pins, then return them to the container.
- For hollow designs, consider placing a wire through the opening to prevent pins from going inside.

For my finisher, I can add about ten small charms or three to four larger pieces at a time. I set the machine nearly at full speed and run it for about ten to fifteen minutes. This works perfectly, almost every time.

Pin finisher barrel with stainless-steel pins. You can skip brass brushing and go right to finishing in the pin finisher, if you'd like.

Liver of sulfur patina is like magic. These designs were patinaed at the same time, and each achieved a different result. And they provide a good view of the colors possible with patina.

APPLYING A PATINA WITH LIVER OF SULFUR GEL

I prefer to use liver of sulfur gel when I patina. I first learned to use liver of sulfur in chunk form and found the gel to be more stable and predictable. I've tried many other patinas on the market, and they all provide great results. I encourage you to try what's available and find your favorite.

Tips for Working with Liver of Sulfur

Liver of sulfur will go through the following color changes: gold, amber, magenta, blue, and black. The intensity of the color changes depends on a number of factors:

- The degree to which the piece has been polished; the higher the initial polish, the brighter the colors.
- Before adding patina, all pieces need to be free of any dirt and oil. For best results, clean your pieces with baking soda and water, especially if they are not fresh from a bath after tumbling.
- Working very carefully, you can add ammonia to the liver of sulfur solution; colors will be more intense and brighter with ammonia.
- You can try other additives such as cola and coffee.
- The temperature of the water and the metal plays a part. The cooler the water, the longer it will take to change color and the duller the colors will be.
- Rinsing your piece after each dip is important to create a finish that lasts.
- Do not immediately place patinaed pieces into the tumbler, since certain tumbling solutions may cause the liver of sulfur patina to bleed, contaminating the water and any other pieces in the tumbler.
- If you are not satisfied with the result or have left your piece inadvertently in the liver of sulfur too long, it is possible to remove the patina entirely by either placing the piece in a kiln to a temp of approximately 1,100°F, or by firing your piece with a butane torch for a few seconds until the patina is gone.

This setup is one I started using while teaching on the road and now use in my own studio. It's so practical since it came from leftovers, it's easy to clean after use, and it stacks well for storage. Shown are an orchid pot, container of liver of sulfur gel, and three reusable plastic containers.

Set up your dunking baths: two containers with very hot (not boiling) water and one with cold water.

Microwave or otherwise heat enough water to fill two of the containers at least 1 inch deep. Fill the third container with cold to room temperature water.

Place liver of sulfur into the other containers with hot water; stir. Repeat until you reach the depth of color you feel yields the amount of patina you desire.

Place all your pieces, especially those that will be in the same design, into the basket and submerge into the first container with hot water. *Patina results vary from bath to bath, so better to get everyone in the pool at the same time, when possible, so your design has a cohesive aesthetic.*

Move the basket from the first container to the container with liver of sulfur.

56 | PROJECTS & TECHNIQUES FOR METAL CLAY JEWELRY

Lift the basket to check the color. Move to the container with cold water.

Repeat the process, moving to the first container to reheat the pieces, then the liver-of-sulfur bath, then the cold water, until you're happy with the color.

When completed, clean the pieces with soap and water. Dispose of the liquids in your garden or suitable disposal location.

If desired, wrap a polishing cloth around a stiff tool and rub across the surface of the design. This will remove patina from raised areas for maximum contrast. Alternatively, you can tumble in silicon carbide mini media, then, for a quick final polish, tumble in a pin finisher.

MECHANICAL POLISHING

You can use an electric polishing machine with a variety of sanding and polishing wheels for all metal studio tasks, including buffing. I prefer the JOOLTOOL for many reasons, including size, variable speed and control, and ease of fume and particulate extraction (not shown in this image).

The JOOLTOOL polisher is used in my studio for all stages of polishing, and then some. Shown here buffing a finished design for one final round of polishing.

TECHNIQUES | 57

Projects

CHAPTER 3

Textured Earrings

A basic, more simple project doesn't have to be basic in design. Even when you're just starting with a new material, you can tailor the design to suit your personal style while pushing your creativity in new directions.

Create this elegant pair of earrings by following a series of techniques: rolling out the clay, texturing, cutting out a simple shape, then creating a few extra elements to dress things up. Applying texture to both sides of clay is optional but does offer a nice finishing touch.

Tools & Materials

- Lump form metal clay
- Prepared embellishments, optional
- Work surface
- Lubricant
- 4- and 3-card gauges
- Non-stick sheet
- Roller
- Textures
- Template or cutter
- Fine-tipped tool
- Paintbrush
- Water dish with water; sponge optional
- Sanding materials
- Finishing tools
- Patina, optional

To complete the design as shown: To an open jumpring, add the top of the earring component and an oval link; close the jumpring. To a second jumpring, add the top of the oval link and the loop of a sterling silver ear thread; close the jumpring.

1. Pretreat your chosen textures. Place a lump of clay onto the prepared area of your work surface.

   Roll the clay out to 4 cards thick, keeping in mind the shape you need for your finished design.

2. Place the clay onto a texture. Then place a 3-card gauge alongside the clay.

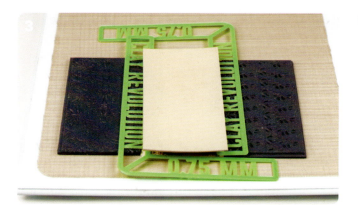

3. Place the second texture on top.

   NOTE: It is important that the measuring gauge is between the textures, so the clay does not get thinner than you intend. If needed, build up the surfaces to equal the dimension of your chosen textures so the gauge is effective.

4. Roll forward across the surface of the uppermost texture.

   TIP: Do this in one motion, if possible, to avoid creating a blurred impression.

5. Remove the top texture, then remove the clay from the lower texture. If you are happy with the impressions, transfer the clay to a non-stick work surface. If you are not happy with the impression, ball up the clay and try again.

6. Using a sharp-tipped tool, cut the clay to the shape of your template. The template used for this design was made by cutting out a piece of scratch foam.

7. Remove any excess clay and wrap it up for later use.

8

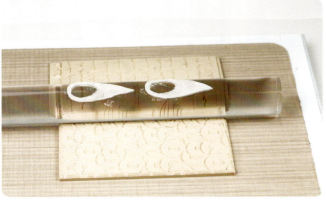

10

8. Use a damp brush to clean up the edges of the clay, including the inside of the hole.

9. If you want to create dimension in your design, carefully transfer the clay to a curved surface.

   Allow the clay to dry completely.

10. Once the clay is dry, refine the clay shape to a nearly perfect finish.

Optional Embellishment

11. Apply a bit of water to the area where you want to add embellishments. Add a bit of water to the underside of the embellishment. The water will help "wake up" the clay.

64 | PROJECTS & TECHNIQUES FOR METAL CLAY JEWELRY

12. Once the water is absorbed, apply a bit of clay paste to each area being joined. Press the two surfaces together and apply light pressure. The paste should "ooze" out, just a bit. As the clay paste dries, the extra will shrink "in" a bit and seal the joint.

13. Once the clay has dried, refine as needed to make the join between the surfaces pristine. Brush any excess clay particles from the surface. Fire the clay to manufacturer's recommended temperature.

14. Once the piece has cooled to room temperature, polish the metal to your desired finish.

    Patina if you'd like.

PROJECTS | 65

CHAPTER 4

Two-Hole Button

Buttons are an essential element in everyday life. That doesn't mean they have to be boring, especially if you have a special sweater you want to personalize or a crocheted scarf that would be perfect with a little something extra.

The buttons in this project are on the easier side to make. Create a textured sheet of clay, cut out your shape (they do not have to be circles!), then add the holes you'll use to attach the button to your garment. For something altogether different, use the button as a clasp in a finished piece of jewelry for a truly one-of-a kind design.

Tools & Materials

- Clay
- Work surface
- Lubricant
- 4- and 3-card gauges
- Non-stick sheet
- Roller
- Texture
- Template or cutter
- Form for shaping
- Fine-tipped tool
- Paintbrush
- Water dish
- Sanding materials
- Finishing tools
- Patina, optional

Finished two-hole buttons stitched onto seed bead woven bracelets

PROJECTS | 67

1. Pretreat your chosen textures. Place a lump of clay onto the prepared area of your work surface.

   Roll the clay out to 4 cards thick, keeping in mind the shape you need for your finished design.

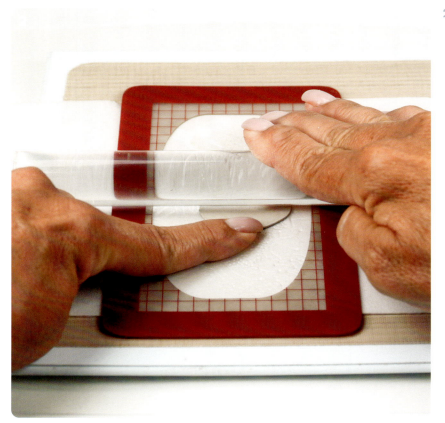

2. Place the clay onto your texture, then place a 3-card gauge alongside the clay. Roll forward across the surface of the clay.

   TIP: *Gently hold the clay at the edge, if needed, to prevent it from sticking to the roller as you press and roll.*

   Once you think you have achieved your desired impression, remove the clay. If you are happy with the impressions, transfer the clay to a non-stick work surface. If you are not happy with the impression, ball up the clay and try again.

3. Place a template onto the surface, exposing the area you want to include in your design. Using a sharp-tipped tool, score the clay along the edge of the template or lightly lubricate the edge of a cutter and press into the clay to cut the shape free.

   Remove any excess clay and wrap up for use later.

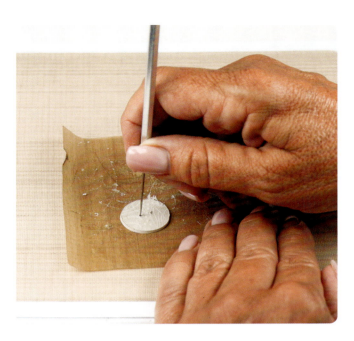

4. Using a sharp-tipped tool, place a pilot hole just off center, to one side. Place a second pilot hole an equal distance from center on the other side.; these will be used to attach your button once complete.

5. Use a damp brush to clean up the edges of the clay, including the edges of the holes you made. Allow the clay to dry completely.

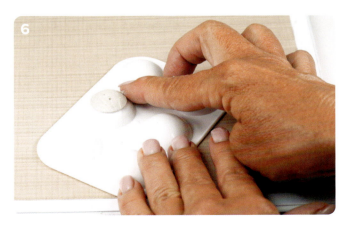

6. Bring some dimension to your button and place onto a curved form. Gently press the edges down to coax it into shape. Allow the clay to dry completely.

7

7. Once the clay is dry, refine the entire surface, using sanding materials. Use a jeweler's file or similar tool to enlarge the pilot holes to be suitable for sewing onto an item later.

   Fire the clay to the manufacturer's recommendation.

8

8. Once the piece is fired and cooled to room temperature, polish the surface to your desired finish.

   Patina if you'd like.

CHAPTER 5

Molded Button with Shank

While teaching a workshop, unrelated to what I was teaching, someone asked me to show them how to use a mold to create a design. It was this leaf design, which I fell in love with.

Soon after returning home, this same person sent me a leaf mold of my very own. These buttons are made as a way to thank for her generosity and kind spirit, and because they are just so pretty, I couldn't keep them to myself!

Form a design using a manufactured mold then transform it with a metal clay bail into a charm or shank button. You can use shank buttons as you would any other button including on clothing, as a decorative touch on a pillow, or as I did here, as a clasp in a jewelry design. The seed beads in this bracelet seem made for these buttons.

Tools & Materials

- Lump form metal clay
- Metal clay paste
- Premade metal clay bail (see "Create a coil from a rope of clay," page 31)
- Work surface
- Premade mold of choice
- Paintbrush
- Water dish
- Sanding materials
- Finishing tools
- Patina, optional

If using a silicone mold, do not add any release agent, since the clay will not easily conform to the mold.

Finished molded shank buttons used as a closure for a right-angle weave seed bead bracelet.

1. Form a lump of clay similar in shape and depth of the mold (this could take a few tries to get right).

   TIP: Weigh the clay as you go to get a sense of how much you need, and keep notes should you want to use the mold again.

2. Place the clay into the cavity of the mold. Press the clay in fully, so you're sure you capture all the details and shape. Remove any excess clay from around the outside edges or any overfill. While working with the clay while it's still fresh, try not to move it around too much once in place, so you preserve the captured texture.

3. OPTIONAL: Apply a texture to the back of the molded shape.

4. Allow the clay to set up. Once set, carefully release the clay from the mold. Allow the clay to dry completely. OPTIONAL: Place the shape onto a form to create dimension.

5. Once the clay is dry, use sanding tools to refine the surface of the clay until it's nearly perfect.

6. Attach a bail to the backside of the design. (For more on how to do this, see "Add a Bail to Create Pendant or Charm," page 32.)

   Allow the clay to dry.

PROJECTS | 75

7. Refine the joint and the surface of the button so it is as near perfect as you can get before firing. Brush the surface of the button to remove any dried clay particles.

   Fire the clay to the manufacturer's recommendation.

8. Once the piece is fired and cooled to room temperature, polish the surface to your desired finish.

   Patina if you'd like.

CHAPTER 6
Layered Bracelet Link

When creating this design, I wanted to bring some dimension to it, so I built in layers with different finished surfaces. I then took the design a little further and curved the layers. Both pieces work well and have their own appeal. Challenge yourself with whichever speaks to you, or make both!

Create the base for a bracelet and apply your favorite texture. Then choose a theme for the layers. Add texture to some of the layers and leave others smooth to really help them stand out.

Tools & Materials

- Lump clay
- Work surface
- Lubricant
- 4- and 3-card gauges
- Non-stick sheet
- Roller
- Textures
- Template and/or cutters
- Fine-tipped tool
- Paintbrush
- Water dish
- Sanding materials
- Finishing tools
- Patina, optional

Finished designs made with layers of metal clay. Each uses the same materials with a little nuance to make bring some dimension. Bracelet on the left is finished with Czech glass beads, beading wire, sterling silver wire guard, crimp beads, and sterling silver lobster clasp. Bracelet on the right is finished with apatite gemstones and sterling silver beads, a fine-silver metal clay oval link, beading wire, sterling silver wire guard, crimp beads, and sterling silver lobster clasp.

1. Pretreat your chosen textures. Place a lump of clay onto the prepared area of your work surface. Place a 4-card gauge on either side of the clay. Using the roller, roll out the clay, turning and flipping as needed to achieve the shape you are looking for. Roll the clay until it meets the height of the gauge.

   NOTE: You don't want the finished version of this component to be thinner than 3 cards thick, since it will be worn as a bracelet. If making it into a pendant, you could consider going thinner.

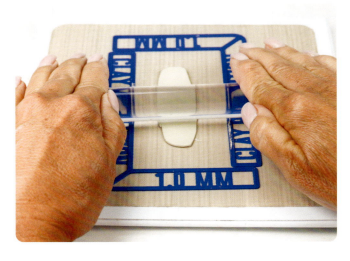

2. Place the clay onto a texture, then place a 3-card gauge alongside the clay. Roll forward across the surface of the clay. If needed, gently hold the edge of the clay so it doesn't roll up onto the roller. Remove the clay from the texture.

   If you are happy with the impressions, transfer the clay to a non-stick work surface. If you are not happy with the impression, ball up the clay and try again.

3. Using a sharp-tipped tool, cut the clay to the shape of your template.

   NOTE: For this design, I wanted to use the same textured clay for some of the layers, so it didn't get wrapped up right away. You can consider doing the same and covering it with cling wrap so you're sure it doesn't dry out before you're ready.

   The template used was cut from scratch foam.

80 | PROJECTS & TECHNIQUES FOR METAL CLAY JEWELRY

4. Cut out openings needed for adding the component to a finished design, later.

5. Use a sharp-tipped tool and template to cut out the pieces needed for your layers.

   To create a layer with a smooth, plain finish, roll a lump of clay to 2 cards thick. Using a template, cut out your desired shape.

6. Use a damp brush to clean up the edges of the clay, including the inside of the openings.

7. Once the clay is dry, refine the clay pieces to a nearly perfect finish.

PROJECTS | 81

8. Apply a bit of water to the area on the bracelet link where you want to add a layer. Add a bit of water to the underside of the first layer. The water will help "wake up" the clay.

9. Once the water is absorbed, apply a bit of clay paste to each surface being joined. Press the two surfaces together and apply light pressure. The paste should "ooze" out, just a bit. As the clay paste dries, the extra will shrink "in" a bit and seal the joint.

   Once the clay has dried again, refine as needed to make the join between the surfaces pristine.

10. Repeat for as many layers as you're adding to your design. Allow to dry fully, then refine as needed with sanding supplies.

11. OPTIONAL: Use clay paste to attach fine-silver granules to the surface. Ensure that you use enough paste so the granules are attached. If not enough paste is used, the paste will shrink in firing and the granules might come free. If too much paste it used, the granules may not stand out as well. It's a balancing act!

    Double-check the overall design and clean up any areas you feel need attention. Brush any excess clay particles from the surface. Fire the clay to manufacturer's recommended temperature.

12

12. Once the piece is cooled to room temperature, polish the metal to your desired finish.

    Patina if you'd like.

13. OPTIONAL: If you want to add dimension to your design, curve the link and the layers before assembly.

    After cutting out your textured link and the holes needed for connecting the link later, place onto a curved surface and allow to dry.

14. After cutting out the layers, place onto a curved surface that provides the height you're looking for.

    Allow the pieces to dry, then refine to near perfection.

PROJECTS | 83

15. Apply water to the areas where you will be joining layers together. Then add a piece of lump clay for adding a bit of distance between the layers or a generous amount of paste so you're sure the layers connect well. There is a lot of room for play here! Apply water to smooth the join between the two layers.

> The particulates you see on the design are left over from the bed of vermiculite the piece was fired in. Vermiculite can be washed away after firing and before final finishing.

16. Dry the piece, then refine with sanding materials until it's nearly perfect. Fire the clay to manufacturer's recommended temperature. Once the piece is cooled to room temperature, polish the metal to your desired finish.

    Patina if you'd like.

Alternate Design

Layered metal clay squares stacked inside each other. Shown on stainless steel wire with stainless steel findings.

PROJECTS | 85

CHAPTER 7

Wrapped Tube Bead and Bail

With this project, the goal is to create a tube bead with a "natural" edge. That is, one created from the natural progression of rolling out the clay. The only tricky part with this design is starting with the right amount of clay and a "log" that expands to the width you want for your bead. It might take a few tries to get it the way you want, but it's worth it!

NOTE: Before you begin, determine the size of tube you want for your bead. Taking the metal clay shrinkage into consideration, choose a mandrel that is about 10 percent larger in diameter than what you want your finished bead to be.

Tools & Materials

- Lump clay
- Clay paste
- Work surface
- Lubricant
- 4- and 3-card gauges
- Non-stick sheet
- Roller
- Texture
- Silicone-tipped tool
- Mandrel (straws were used for this design)
- Paintbrush
- Water dish with water; sponge optional
- Sanding materials
- Finishing tools
- Patina, optional

Create a tube bead, then use it in a finished design like any other bead. Following the same process, take the bead a step further and turn it into a bail. You can use the bail like a bead or pendant, then add a bead or charm from the loop you add.

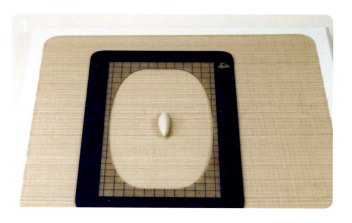

1. Prepare your tools and area. Pinch off a lump of clay and form into a thin log, with a middle that is wider than the ends.

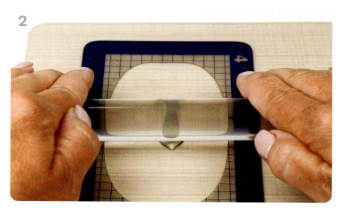

2. Place the clay onto your work surface and roll to a 4-card thickness. The log should elongate with tapered ends.

3. Place this sheet of clay onto your texture. Roll to a 3-card thickness. The clay should further elongate and be about ¾" longer than the straw's circumference.

4. Pick up the clay and center it on the straw.

TIP: Loosely wrap the ends together so one overlaps the other to ensure the fit. If too long, you may want to start over, removing the extra clay.

5. Once you like the fit, turn the assembly upside down. Flip the end that will be on top away from the straw. With a paintbrush, apply water to the top surface on the end still wrapped against the straw and the underside of the end that is open and away from the straw.

88 | PROJECTS & TECHNIQUES FOR METAL CLAY JEWELRY

6.

7.

6. Wrap the free end back over the clay wrapped around the straw. Apply pressure to secure the layers together.

7. Hold for a few seconds and until you're sure the ends are joined, then set the assembly aside, resting the straw so the clay is suspended. This will ensure the clay stays round and doesn't develop a flat spot.

Allow the clay to sit until you're sure the shape will hold, then remove from the straw. If you start to remove the tube and feel the clay giving to your pressure, allow more time for the shape to set up.

Once you can free the tube from the straw, set the tube aside so the clay can dry fully. If you wait until the clay is fully dry, it could be hard to remove the clay from the form. A straw will yield and compress, so won't be a problem, but keep this in mind for other forms.

PROJECTS | 89

8. Dry the piece, then refine with sanding materials until it's nearly perfect. Fire the clay to manufacturer's recommended temperature.

9. Once the piece is cooled to room temperature, polish the metal to your desired finish.

   Patina if you'd like.

10. Using the same tools and materials, plus a premade metal clay bail (see "Create a coil from a rope of clay," page 31), follow the instructions for creating a bead. Once the bead is dried and finished to nearly perfect, add a premade bail. (For more on how to do this, see "Add a bail to create a pendant or charm," page 32.)

11. Dry the piece, then refine with sanding materials until it's nearly perfect. Fire the clay to manufacturer's recommended temperature.

    Once the piece is cooled to room temperature, polish the metal to your desired finish.

    Patina if you'd like.

Alternate Design

Tube bead bracelet is made with leather cording, lampworked bead by Aja Vaz, metal clay acorn charm, metal clay textured charm, sterling silver, end caps, and lobster clasp.

Alternate Design

Tube bead bail is strung on a Viking knit chain. From the bail a metal clay starfish button with shank, lampwork bead by Amber Higgins of Worn Beadies, and textured metal clay charm are added with sterling silver wire. From the end caps a lampwork bead by Amber Higgins is strung from fine-silver wire headpin along with sterling silver beads.

PROJECTS | 91

CHAPTER 8
Masked Textured Pendant

This design concept was born from my love of bringing all my interests together and finding new ways to use the materials I have. I love working with textures, and one day, I had stencils nearby and thought it would be cool to add texture in the pattern of a stencil. It took a lot of trial and error to find the right stencil and texture combination, but when I did, I was in love with the results.

This design can be made in any format or shape and used in unlimited ways. You can choose to use a simple bail on top as well as to hang the charm—I had started out that way, then changed to the more organic option you see in the finished design, just to change things up and soften the triangle, as if it's been lost in time and covered in vines.

I chose the smooth rondelle shape to contrast with the texture and all the other movements this pendant has going on—faceted stones were just too much. To complement the edginess, I felt that a dark-color gemstone was the only way to go, so I chose chrome diopside but almost went with black spinel. The heavier chain was the perfect finishing option for me.

Tools & Materials

- Lump Clay
- Syringe-type clay (optional)
- Premade metal clay bail (see "Create a coil from a rope of clay," page 31)
- Work surface
- Lubricant
- 5- and 4-card gauges
- Non-stick sheet
- Roller
- Textures
- Stencil
- Fine-tipped tool
- Paintbrush
- Water dish
- Sanding materials
- Finishing tools
- Patina, optional

1. When choosing your own texture and stencil options—I recommend starting with a texture that has a smaller, tighter format and a stencil with clearly defined patterns and nothing with thin lines, or the texture might not be obvious enough to be impactful. As you explore the possibilities, you'll get your own feel for what works best for you.

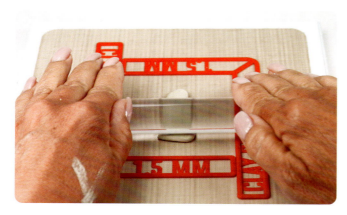

2. Pretreat your chosen textures. Place a lump of clay onto the prepared area of your work surface. Place a 5-card gauge on either side of the clay. Roll out the clay, turning and flipping as needed to be close to the shape you are looking for. Roll the clay until it meets the height of the gauge.

3. Place a 3-card stack on either side of the clay, then place a stencil over the clay.

94 | PROJECTS & TECHNIQUES FOR METAL CLAY JEWELRY

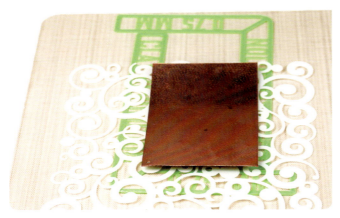

4. Place a texture on top of the stencil, face down. Press firmly or roll across the surface.

   TIP: If you're using a metal texture like I did here, you may find that burnishing the surface with your hands versus rolling across with a roller will yield better results.

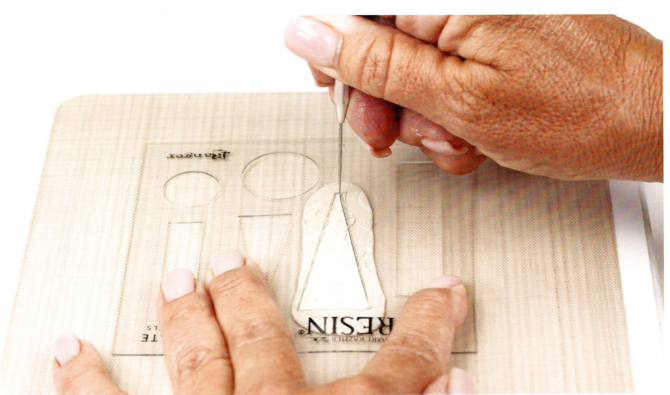

5. Remove the texture and the stencil, then transfer to a non-stick sheet. Using a cutter or a template and fine-tipped tool, cut out your desired shape. Use a damp paintbrush to clean up the edges, then allow the clay to dry.

   OPTIONAL: Repeat to create a charm to complement the design.

6. Once the clay is dry, refine the surface until the designs are nearly perfect.

PROJECTS | 95

7

7. Using a paintbrush, apply water where you will be adding a bail for hanging the pendant from. Using syringe-type clay, "draw" out a bail to suit your design. Apply water and gentle pressure to ensure the two surfaces are joined. Once the water absorbs, use a damp paintbrush, stylus, or similar tool to refine the shape as needed. Allow the design to sit undisturbed until the clay is dry.

Add a bail for the charm. (For more on how to do this, see "Add a Bail to Create a Pendant or Charm," page 32.) Allow the fresh clay to dry, then refine the surface.

Refine the bail and surrounding area until the design is nearly perfect. Dust off any stray particles of clay "dust." Fire the clay to the manufacturer's recommendation.

8

8. Once the piece is fired and cooled to room temperature, polish the surface to your desired finish.

   Patina if you'd like.

Alternate Designs

Add your components to any finished piece of jewelry.

A • Using jumprings, add a length of chain to a component, then finish with a lobster clasp.

B • Using cord ends, adhesive, and jumprings, connect a piece of leather for the finishing touch.

C • Using jumprings, create a chain-maille design that complements the masked texture; finish with a sterling silver lobster clasp.

PROJECTS | 97

CHAPTER 9

Large Hook Bracelet

This design idea came about when my Aunt Barbara asked for something different. I went out of the box and came up with this concept. She loved it and still wears it to this day, as do all the other family members who have one.

The original design was made with a smooth surface and a design "drawn" on in syringe-type clay. Alternatively, you can make the design with texture. If working with a texture, start with a thicker layer of clay and work no thinner than a final layer of 4 cards thick.

The tab clasp can get be rolled to a final layer of 3 cards thick. Note that the dimension of the tab can get a bit clunky, since the opening needs to be as wide as the widest part of the hook. I don't mind the way these turned out, but you could always taper the hook to be thinner than the main part of the design and adjust the tab size, accordingly.

Tools & Materials

- Lump clay
- Syringe-type clay
- Work surface
- Lubricant
- 5-, 4- and 3-card gauges
- Non-stick sheet
- Roller
- Templates
- Small cutter
- Small mandrel
- Forming tool
- Pencil
- Fine-tipped tool
- Paintbrush
- Water dish with water; sponge optional
- Sanding materials
- Finishing tools
- Patina, optional
- Texture, optional

Hook-style component clasped with a tab closure can be connected to any type of material. Shown here with faceted gemstone beads that complement the seahorse. Other designs: hook-style bracelets finished with sterling silver round beads in a range of sizes.

PROJECTS | 99

Templates

Copy these illustrations to a scale that suits the size of your wrist. I transfered the hook and tab shapes to a piece of scratch foam to use as a template when cutting the wet clay. I cut the seahorse from copy paper then traced around the outline directly onto the dried clay, using a pencil.

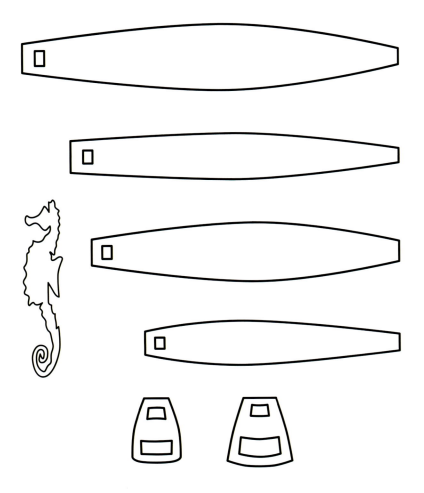

1. Pretreat your work surface and tools. Place a log of clay onto the prepared area of your work surface. Roll out to 4 cards thick.

2. Transfer the clay to a non-stick sheet. Place a template onto the surface of the clay and cut out the shape, using a sharp-tipped tool. Wrap up any excess clay for use later.

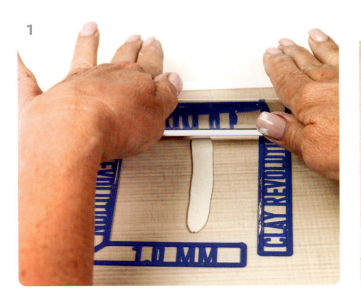
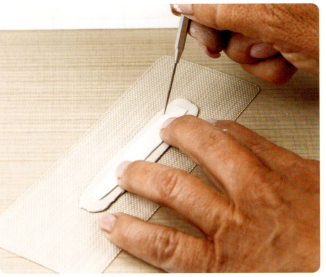

3. Use the small cutter to remove clay from the narrow end. This opening will be used to anchor your stringing material, later.

4. Wrap the other end of the clay around a straw or other suitable mandrel to form the hook. Carefully place the clay onto or into a form. The direction you place the clay depends on the form you're using and how the clay needs to be shaped to keep the hook in the right formation and direction.

5. Roll a fresh piece of clay out to 3 or 4 cards thick. Cut out the tab template. Clean up the cut edges with a paintbrush and a bit of water. Set the clay aside to dry.

6. Refine both pieces to near perfect.

7. OPTIONAL: Use a template to sketch a design on the face of the hook.

8. Wet the area where you will be applying the syringe-type clay. Allow the water to absorb.

9. Apply syringe-type clay as neatly as you can.

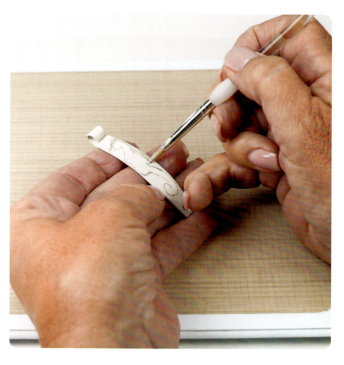

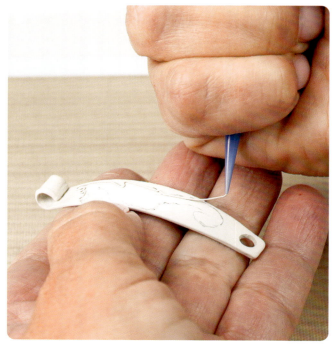

10. Flood the area with water, then gently press the fresh clay so it connects with the surface of the hook. (For more on working with syringe-type clay, see "Syringe Tips," page 40.)

    Allow the clay to dry undisturbed.

    NOTE: The water you added might soften the clay of the hook, so be careful not to flex the curve, if possible.

11. Refine the surface of both parts so they are as near perfect as you can get before firing. Double-check that the syringe design is connected to the base clay. If needed, add more clay, dry, and refine again. Once complete, brush the surface to remove any dried clay particles.

    Fire the clay to manufacturer's recommendation.

    Once the piece is fired and cooled to room temperature, polish the surface to your desired finish.

    Patina if you'd like.

PROJECTS | 103

CHAPTER 10

Toggle Clasp

"Form follows function—function and form are one:" the teachings of architect Louis H. Sullivan further amplified by Frank Lloyd Wright.

We need findings to finish our jewelry designs. They have a function, and at their core, the function requires only rudimentary design. In many finished jewelry designs, the findings--including clasp--are hidden or down played. A toggle clasp has no business being front and center or anything more than made to hold two ends of a necklace together. In this design, we make the toggle a significant focal point and allow it to be substantial (more than is needed) and beautiful.

Tools & Materials

- Lump form metal clay
- Metal clay paste
- Premade metal clay bail (2) (see "Create a coil from a rope of clay," page 31)
- Work surface
- Lubricant
- 6- and 4-card gauges
- Non-stick sheet
- Roller
- Textures
- Templates or cutters
- Fine-tipped tool
- Paintbrush
- Water dish with water; sponge optional
- Sanding materials
- Finishing tools
- Patina, optional

The toggle clasp in this necklace is integrated as part of the design and works alongside the other design elements—it is not just a clasp. The necklace includes sterling silver, Czech glass beads, lampwork beads by Aja Vaz, raku pendant by Marianne Kasparian of Maku Raku, beading wire, wire guards, crimp beads, and crimp covers.

1. Pretreat your chosen texture. Place a lump of clay onto the prepared area of your work surface.

   Roll the clay out to 6 cards thick, keeping in mind the shape you need for your finished design.

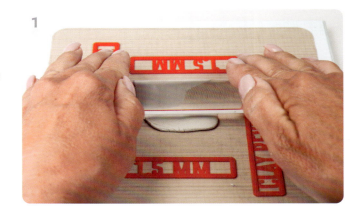

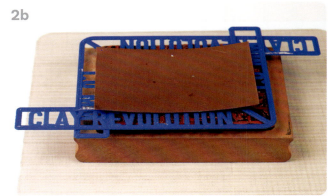

2. Place the clay onto a texture, then place another texture on top. Be sure to place 4-card gauges in between the textures so the clay is rolled out to the correct and an even thickness.

   TIP: When using a metal texture, I often default to pressing and rubbing the back of the texture plate versus using a roller. When using a roller, it usually gets away from me and flies across the room.

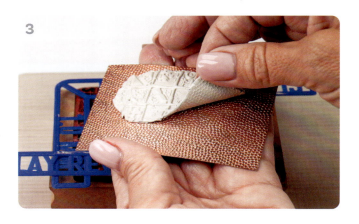

3. Remove the clay from the texture. If you are happy with the impressions, transfer the clay to a non-stick work surface. If you are not happy with the impression, ball up the clay and try again.

4. Using a cutter or sharp-tipped tool, cut the clay to shape. Remove any excess clay and wrap up for later use.

106 | PROJECTS & TECHNIQUES FOR METAL CLAY JEWELRY

5. Place a smaller cutter or template into the center and press firmly. Remove the center cut-out section and save to make into a charm, if you want. Otherwise, combine it with the other leftover clay.

6. Use a damp paintbrush to clean up and smooth the cut edges.

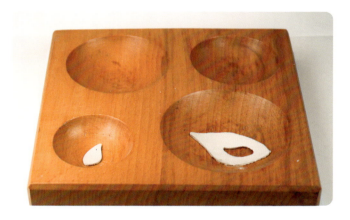

7. Set the cut-out shape aside. Shape in a form if you want to add some dimension to your toggle. While the toggle is drying, create the toggle bar.

   Form a log of clay and place on your clean work surface. Using a rectangular piece of acrylic, begin rolling the clay into a thinner log, long enough to extend past the widest part of the cut-out section of the toggle. The toggle bar needs to extend past the toggle opening so it doesn't slip through when worn.

   Set the bar aside to dry.

8. Refine all areas of the toggle and the toggle bar.

9. Once the toggle parts are nearly perfect, attach a bail to the back of the toggle and one along the length of the toggle bar. (For more on how to do this, see "Add a Bail to Create Pendant or Charm," page 32.) These will be used to connect your stringing material. Connect to each half, following instructions.

   Once the clay pieces are dry, refine them so they are nearly perfect before firing.

10. Refine the joint and the surface of the toggle and bar so they are as near perfect as you can get before firing. Brush the surface to remove any dried clay particles.

    Fire the clay to manufacturer's recommendation. Once fired and cooled to room temperature, polish the surface to your desired finish.

    Patina if you'd like.

108 | PROJECTS & TECHNIQUES FOR METAL CLAY JEWELRY

Alternate Designs

The toggles shown here are made to a thickness of 4 cards at their thinnest. You can work to no thinner than 3 cards, if you'd like, but these are intended to be large and hold a lot of weight as well as be a focal point in your design.

Left: A square cutter was used for this toggle. The corners were rounded to form a pleasing and comfortable design. A smaller square was cut from inside the shape to allow the toggle bar to pass through. Three small square holes were cut from the shape to later be used for stringing a multi-strand design. The toggle bar was textured using the same texture mat as the toggle, and a metal clay bail was added to connect the other ends of the design.

Right: A fun "cookie" cutter was used for the toggle shape and a complementary cake-decorating cutter used for the center opening. A metal clay bail was used on the underside for connecting the design. The toggle bar was kept simple and also has a metal clay bail for finishing the ends of a design.

PROJECTS | 109

CHAPTER 11
Molded Shell Pendant

The finished design shown is made using a silicone mold made from an ethically sourced conical shell. When sourcing materials for your own design, be sure to check local regulations before removing shells, rocks, or similar from the area. See "Creating a Two-Part Silicone Mold" on page 43 before beginning this project. NOTE: When using a silicone mold, do not add any release agent, since the clay will resist conforming to the mold, making it hard to capture the design.

Tools & Materials

- Metal clay lump form
- Work surface
- Premade mold of choice
- Smooth acrylic sheet or similar
- Paintbrush
- Water dish
- Sanding materials
- Finishing tools
- Patina, optional

This pendant design stands up well on its own, so it is strung simply on a cable necklace.

1. Form a lump of clay similar in shape to the mold, so there will be some depth once fitted into place inside the mold. This could take a few tries to get right. Weigh the clay as you go to get a sense of how much you need, and keep notes should you want to use the mold again.

2. Place the clay into the cavity of the mold.

3. Press the clay in fully, so you're sure you capture all the details and shape.

112 | PROJECTS & TECHNIQUES FOR METAL CLAY JEWELRY

4. OPTIONAL: Place the item you used to create the mold against the back of the clay to add texture and form. Remove any excess clay from around the outside edges or any overfill.

5. Allow the clay to set up. Once set, release from the mold. Carefully remove the cast clay from the item if you used one to add additional relief and shape.

   Allow the clay to dry completely.

6. Once the clay is dry, use sanding tools to refine the surface of the clay until it's nearly perfect.

PROJECTS | 113

7. Using the acrylic sheet, roll clay into a long rope. You will want to work as quickly as possible, since the clay dries more readily when in this thin form.

   Anchor one end of the rope onto the molded clay, then wind around into a pleasing form, creating the bail to be used for hanging the pendant.

8. Anchor the second end. Trim any excess clay.

   Apply a bit of water to the areas where the clay is anchored to the molded clay and where it touches itself; apply pressure to seal these areas, securing them together and creating strength in the connection.

   Allow the clay to dry.

9. Refine the joints and the surface of the pendant so it is as nearly perfect as you can get it.

114 | PROJECTS & TECHNIQUES FOR METAL CLAY JEWELRY

10. Roll a new rope of clay, thin enough that it can fit through the bail you created on top of your design. Feed the rope through the opening twice, if possible, forming a bail to use for stringing your design and one that is complementary to your pendant.

    Using a paintbrush, apply water to the new bail in the area where the clay ends touch other fresh clay. Use a silicone-tipped tool to smooth the ends into other areas of the fresh clay, securing the layers and forming a secure connection.

    NOTE: Do your best **not** to connect the fresh clay to the dried clay. If you inadvertently do, work carefully to break the connection before firing. If you fire the finished design with connections you don't want, you risk them being fired together.

    Dry the clay, then refine to a nearly perfect state. Brush the entire surface to remove any dried clay particles.

    Fire the clay to the manufacturer's recommendation.

11. Once the piece is fired and cooled to room temperature, polish the surface to your desired finish.

    Patina if you'd like.

PROJECTS | 115

CHAPTER 12
Seed Pod Earrings

The finished design shown is made using rose campion or Lychnis Atrosanguinea pods. You can recreate this design using pods from the same plant or others found in your area. The options for this type of design can include anything safe to fire in a kiln—which is anything organic, such as crackers, cereal, plant matter, etc. Plastic or similar would not be recommended for this type of design, since the fumes would be toxic. If you'd like to cast a design using something not suitable for firing, consider creating a silicone mold and following the instructions found on page 43.

NOTE: It is recommended that this type of design be fired in a kiln rather than using a torch.

Tools & Materials

- Metal clay lump form
- Metal clay paste form
- Work surface
- Acrylic sheet
- Non-stick sheet
- Silicone-tipped tool
- Paintbrush
- Water dish with water; sponge optional
- Fine-tipped awl
- Sanding materials
- Finishing tools
- Patina, optional
- Organic item to be cast in clay

Finished earrings hung on fine-silver wire suspended from sterling silver earwires

1. Stir the paste-type clay, using the handle of your paintbrush, bamboo skewer, or other similar item. You want to make sure you stir the paste, working all the way to the bottom of the jar, incorporating any silver particles that may have settled on the bottom.

   Using a paintbrush, apply a thin coat of paste-type clay to the entire surface of the pod, getting into all areas and a little up the stem. Set onto a non-stick worksheet to allow it to dry.

2. Repeat six more times. You will notice the object getting heavier.

3. Repeat to create as many organic items as you'd like in your design. Once items are dry, refine to create a near-perfect finish.

4. Pinch off about 10 grams from the package of clay and roll it into a cylindrical shape. Using an acrylic rolling rectangle, roll across the clay, stretching it into a thin rope with one end tapered. For more on this technique, see "Rolling a Rope of Clay" on page 29.

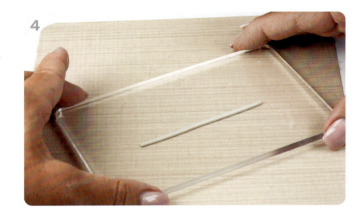

5. Attach the thinner end of the rope along the side of the pod, so the tip almost touches the end where the petals were. Wind the clay up and around the stem the form into a loop at the top. You will use the loop to suspend the pod, so keep that in mind when you shape and create an opening in the center.

6. Use a silicone-tipped tool to smooth the tapered end into place, giving it a graduated effect.

7. Apply water to all the areas where the clay touches itself and along the dried pod. This will create contact points and provide structure and strength.

   Allow the clay to dry undisturbed.

8. Carefully refine the dried clay until you are pleased with the finish of your pod and branch.

   TIP: Be sure to refine the points on the end of the pod so they don't poke you when wearing your pendant.

   Brush the entire surface to remove any dried clay particles.

9. Fire the clay to the manufacturer's recommendation. Once the piece is fired and cooled to room temperature, polish the surface to your desired finish.

   Patina if you'd like.

Alternate Designs

These were made using the following organic materials:

A • Rose of Sharon pods
B • Acorns
C • A river birch branch

PROJECTS | 121

CHAPTER 13

Hollow Lentil Earrings

Lentils are so fun to make but do present a few challenges. Once you have a formula for a finished size you like, write down the thickness you rolled to, the size circle you cut out, and the doming form you used.

I prefer a lentil with a bit of depth, so I start with clay that is thicker by one more card than it really needs to be. Then, when I cut out the circle, I find the right size doming form, so the edges of the clay are facing down rather than flaring out. This yields a better depth to the lentil.

Tools & Materials

- Metal clay lump form
- Metal clay paste form
- Lubricant
- Textures
- 5- and 4-card gauges
- Roller
- Template and fine-tipped tool
- Circle cutters in a few sizes
- Paintbrush
- Water dish with water; sponge optional
- Non-stick sheet
- Doming form
- Sanding materials
- Finishing tools
- Pencil
- Optional: centering device, patina

Finished earrings hung on a sterling silver chain suspended from sterling silver earwires

1. Pretreat your chosen textures. Place a lump of clay onto the prepared area of your work surface.

   Roll the clay out to 5 cards thick, keeping in mind the shape you need for your finished design.

   Transfer the clay to a texture mat. Roll the clay to a 4-card thickness.

2. Transfer the textured clay to a non-stick sheet. Use a circle cutter or circle template and fine-tipped tool to cut out the circle. The circle for this design is 7/8 inch.

   Use a paintbrush and a bit of water to clean the edge of the metal clay.

3. Transfer the cut clay to a doming form, so the clay dries with a curved surface. Ensure the clay is formed to the surface, including the edges.

4. Remove the clay from the drying form.

   Place one circle on a sanding sheet. Apply pressure and use a figure-eight motion as you move a circle across the sanding surface, removing clay evenly from the inside rim, only. The figure-eight motion ensures you're putting even pressure across the entire surface.

   NOTE: *Check frequently, since you don't want to remove too much material but do need it to be smooth and even across the entire edge. Also ensure the thickness along the edge is even; sometimes the texture causes some areas to be thicker than others, so do your best to create an equal, even thickness along the edge as well as a flat, even inside rim.*

   Repeat for all circles.

5. Pair two circles up that match the best.

   While holding the domed circles together, rotate them around to find the best fit. Mark the edges so you can pair them up at the same point, later. A pencil mark at three points works well.

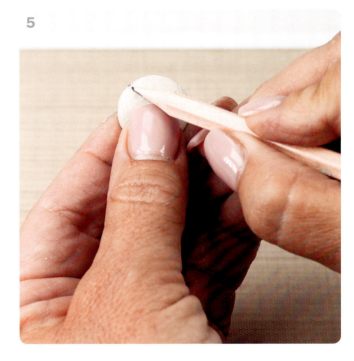

6. Use a paintbrush to apply a bit of water to the inside rim of each circle. Allow the water to absorb. Then, apply a bead of metal clay paste to each rim. Line up the registration marks, then press the two halves together. Hold for a few seconds before setting aside to dry completely.

   Excess paste will "ooze" out; this is okay, but if it's excessive, you can use a damp brush to remove some.

PROJECTS | 125

7

7. Refine the outside edge so the circle is cleaned up and in good shape.

    Repeat for a second lentil if creating a pair.

8

8. Use a centering device to find the center of one lentil. Make a mark.

9

9. At the mark, carefully use a jeweler's file to make a hole. You will need to apply pressure, and, at this size, the lentil should be sturdy, but you do not want to press so hard that you collapse your dome.

    Flip the lentil over and repeat on the other side. Once you have a hole on each side of the lentil, pass a needle tool all the way through and spin the lentil to assess balance. If needed, adjust the hole so the lentil hangs straight and evenly.

    Repeat to create the hole in the second lentil.

    Refine the entire shape of the lentil, using the polishing papers, working through the progressive grits.

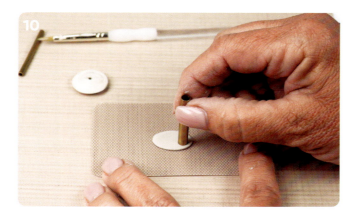

10. OPTIONAL: Create a clay "donut" to dress the center opening.

    Assess the center opening on the lentil. Choose a circle cutter that is about 3 mm larger than the hole.

    Choose a smaller circle cutter that is equal to or about 1 mm larger than the hole.

    Roll out a small lump of clay to 2 cards thick. Using the larger of the two circle cutters, cut out one circle.

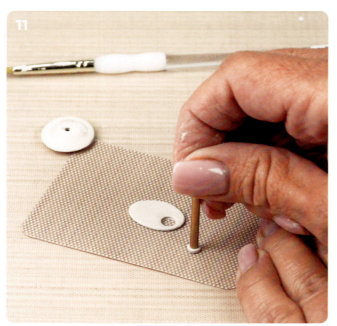

11. Center the smaller circle cutter on the cutout and cut out the center.

12. Wet the area around the hole on one side of one lentil. Allow the water to absorb, apply some paste to the "donut," and apply to the surface of the lentil, adjusting the placement so it's centered on the lentil. Allow to dry.

    Repeat for each side of each lentil.

PROJECTS | 127

13. Refine the lentils so they are as close to perfect as you can make them.

    Fire the clay to manufacturer's recommendation.

14. Once the earrings are fired and cooled to room temperature, polish the surface to your desired finish.

    Patina if you'd like.

Alternate Designs

The top "bead" was made with a larger circle draped over a form that allowed the sides to fall far. When joining two circles formed this way, it was possible to join them to create a much more voluminous design.

The other lentils were formed the same as the lentils in the project, but holes were added above the center line so they could be strung on a cable and hang correctly as a pendant. The edges of the openings were finished with clay donuts.

CHAPTER 14

Abstract Brooch

Brooches come in and out of fashion, but I say there is always room for a brooch whether on a denim jacket, blazer, knitted or woven scarf, or even a hat! Creating a brooch design can be much like painting on a canvas. It can be any size, shape, or form and can contain a variety of design elements.

This project's design came after some time. I assembled an assortment of textures and stamps and just let them sit by my side while I worked on other designs. I like to have things nearby and available for when the right moment strikes. (Yes, that means there is a veritable mess around me all the time--but I don't see a mess, only possibility!)

Dina Wakley's stamp caught my eye (how could you not be captivated by that face?!), and then it was a matter of working fast enough to capture the vision that came to me for where this design was headed.

Tools & Materials

- Metal clay lump form
- Metal clay paste form (optional)
- Work surface
- Lubricant
- 4-, 3-, and 2-card gauges
- Non-stick sheet
- Roller
- Textures
- Stamp, cling-stamp base, if needed
- Fine-tipped tool
- Paintbrush
- Water dish
- Sanding materials
- Finishing tools
- Patina, optional

Abstract brooch design inspired by Dina Wakley's stamp from her series, The Littles, distributed by Ranger Ink. The background is Floral, a texture mat designed by Barbara Becker-Simon.

1. Pretreat your chosen stamp and texture. Place a lump of clay onto the prepared area of your work surface. Roll the clay out to 3-card thickness, turning and flipping as needed to achieve the shape you are looking for.

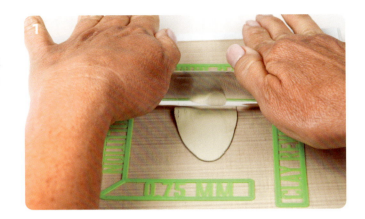

2. Place the clay onto a non-stick sheet. Place the stamp onto the surface of the clay and press. In this case, the clay cannot get too thin with this stamp; in fact, the stamp will help impress the cut lines and make it easier to trim, later. If using a texture mat, place 2-card gauges on the mat so you don't make the clay too thin.

   Remove the stamp. If you are happy with the impressions, proceed. If you are not happy with the impression, ball up the clay and try again.

3. Using a sharp-tipped tool, cut the clay to the shape you'd like for your design.

4. Using a paintbrush and water, smooth the cut edges. Set aside to dry.

5. Roll a fresh piece of clay to 4 cards thick. Place the clay onto the texture mat and roll to 3 cards thick.

6. Place the stamped, dried clay onto the fresh textured sheet, to help with the design and knowing where to cut the sheet. Use a sharp-tipped tool to cut out the pieces needed for your base layer.

   Remove the dried pieces of clay. Use a damp brush to clean up the edges of the fresh clay.

7. Once the clay is dry, refine the clay pieces to a nearly perfect finish.

8. Apply a bit of water to the area where you will join the layers. Add a bit of water to the underside of the top layer.

9. Once the water is absorbed, apply a bit of clay or clay paste to the surface being joined. Press the two surfaces together and apply light pressure. The clay should "ooze" out, just a bit. As the clay dries, the extra will shrink "in" a bit and seal the joint.

   Once the clay has dried again, refine as needed to make the join between the surfaces pristine.

   NOTE: I used lump clay to join the layers together in this design to make sure the join was secure. Clay paste will work just as well; you just might have to add more paste to fill in gaps.

10. Repeat for as many layers as you're adding to your design. Allow to dry fully, then refine as needed with sanding supplies.

    Apply the brooch findings so they are secure. (For more on how to do this, see "Attaching Fine Silver Findings," page 48.)

11. Refine to a nearly perfect finish. Fire the clay to manufacturer's recommendation. Once it's fired and cooled to room temperature, polish the surface to your desired finish.

    Once the brooch is cooled to room temperature, polish the metal to your desired finish.

    Patina if you'd like.

12. Add the pin to the finding.

CHAPTER 15
Circle Chain Links

When setting out to make a chain, I reminded myself what I tell others when leading a workshop. "Metal clay has its benefits and should be played to its strengths. Unless you have no choice, don't set out to use metal clay to replicate something that already exists, and in a less expensive form such as fine or sterling silver round wire and metal sheet." So, I sat with my interest in making a chain for a while.

When gathering materials for other projects, I found a mold I had not used in a long time and thought I'd give it a try. That is how this design was born.

As I made the links, like it is with the lentils, you need to find the right thickness for the clay, the right size circle to cut out (in this case, the right size center circle to cut out), and the right size mold to create the right curve, for it to all come together. I'll share the sizes I used, but I encourage you to play and find your own favorites.

When putting the design together, the oval links made from the embellishment molds were the perfect accompaniment.

Tools & Materials

- Metal clay lump form
- Lubricant
- Textures
- 4- and 3-card gauges
- Roller
- Circle template and fine-tipped tool or circle cutters in a few sizes
- Silicone mold
- Paintbrush
- Water dish with water; sponge optional
- Non-stick sheet
- Doming form
- Stylus
- Sanding materials
- Finishing tools
- Pencil
- OPTIONAL:
- Centering device
- Ceramic stone polishing bit, burr, or similar
- Patina

Circle chain-link necklace includes links made from the instructions in this chapter, oval links made following the instructions in "Creating Embellishments from Manufactured Molds" on page 46, and sterling silver jumprings.

1. Pretreat your chosen textures. Place a lump of clay onto the prepared area of your work surface.

   Roll the clay out to 4 cards thick, keeping in mind the shape you need for your finished design.

2. Transfer the clay to a texture sheet. Roll the clay to a 3-card thickness.

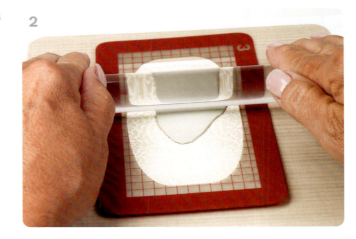

3. Transfer the textured clay to a non-stick sheet. Use a circle cutter or circle template and fine-tipped tool to cut out the circle.

   Circle sizes shown in this project:
   - 1 3/8" with a 3/8" center hole
   - 1 1/8" with a 21/64" center hole
   - 3/4" with a 7/32" center hole

138 | PROJECTS & TECHNIQUES FOR METAL CLAY JEWELRY

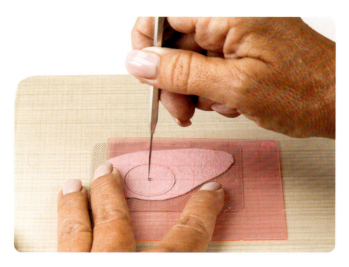

4. Place a centering device over the circle you just cut, and make a mark.

5. Place the template over the mark and center the circle. Use the fine-tipped tool to cut out the center. Gather then wrap up the excess clay. *NOTE: As you continue to place things on top of the original circle, you may inadvertently press the clay back together; recut the original circle as needed.*

6. Transfer the circle to the silicone mold and place into the doming form. Gently press the circle down into the form.

7. Dip the tip of a medium-size ball stylus into the water. Gently press the surface of the stylus against the clay to help seat it better in the mold.

PROJECTS | 139

8. *NOTE: Do not use too much water or too much pressure or you might lose the texture.*

9. Allow the clay to dry. Then remove it from the mold.

10. Refine the entire surface, playing close attention to the edges, including the edges along the center cutout. Make sure they are smooth and even.

140 | PROJECTS & TECHNIQUES FOR METAL CLAY JEWELRY

11. Make a mark at the center point between the edge of the center opening and outside edge. Then make a second mark directly opposite the first.

    TIP: *When planning how you will use the circles, choose where to place the marks based on how the circles will hang. In the necklace on page 136, the center link has holes placed above center, so it hangs correctly. The circle made for the toggle ring will only have one hole.*

12. At the mark, carefully use a jeweler's file to make a hole. Use pressure as you maneuver the file, and clean away the clay debris from time to time. Keep in mind the clay is fragile at this stage, so work slowly. If you try to force the file too quickly, the clay could give in to the pressure and break.

13. To further refine the circle, use a ceramic grinding bit or burr to refine the holes made from the jeweler's files. Just a little twist or two will refine the opening.

    Brush the surface to remove any dried clay particles.

14. Fire the clay to manufacturer's recommendation. Once the clay has been fired and cooled to room temperature, polish the surface to your desired finish.

PROJECTS | 141

15. If you're using a circle as part of a toggle clasp, make a toggle bar.

    Form a log of clay and place on your clean work surface. Using a rectangular piece of acrylic, begin rolling the clay into a thinner log, long enough to extend past the widest part of the cutout section of the toggle. *NOTE: The toggle bar needs to extend past the toggle opening so it doesn't slip through when worn.*

    Set the bar aside to dry.

16. Refine all areas of the toggle bar.

    Once the toggle bar is nearly perfect, attach a bail. (For more on how to do this, see "Add a Bail to Create Pendant or Charm," page 32.)

    Once the clay pieces are dry, refine them so they are nearly perfect before firing.

    Fire the clay to the manufacturer's recommendation. Once the piece is fired and cooled to room temperature, polish the surface to your desired finish.

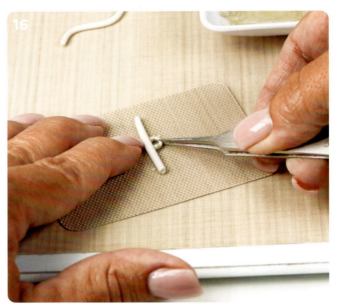

17. Patina if you'd like. *NOTE: These pieces were done as an example. I recommend adding patina to the finished design at one time, so you get the most consistent results for the whole piece.*

142 | PROJECTS & TECHNIQUES FOR METAL CLAY JEWELRY

Alternate Designs

Circle chain-link bracelet and earrings. The earrings are hung from sterling silver wire, 21-gauge, half hard. The bracelet circles are connected using links made from a mold and sterling silver 16-gauge jumprings.

PROJECTS | 143

Acknowledgments

This book would not be possible if it weren't for the endless love and support my family provides me. Their tolerance of my absence when I'm traveling and when I'm head down and distracted working on projects I'm so passionate to create (like this book). For always turning a blind eye to the tools and materials I have taken over our house with. For your acceptance of who I am. I love you all with every fiber of my being. Without you there would be no joy.

Reaching the point in my journey where I can write a book would not be possible if it weren't for the support I received when first starting this creative path. The endless encouragement; early days of selling my polymer clay pins, pens, and kaleidoscopes; the endless excitement when I shared something new (even if you had no idea what I was going on about); and for never telling me I couldn't reach that next goal—thank you.

For the woman who gave me a chance and said, "You can do what I can't, and I can do what you can't, and together we can accomplish anything." Thank you, Merle for believing in me when I interviewed to be an editor with scant experience and a lot of heart and passion. Thank you for finding the resources needed for equipment to improve our published projects, and so I could take classes making me a better editor. This has all led to a lifelong passion as a maker and instructor, at a level I never knew was possible. Thank you for allowing me to pitch what became Bead Fest, even though we were already at our max—what a dream come true and what a ride it was to bring it to life. Thank you for being you and for helping me become a better version of myself.

To those who, even after 30+years, ask to see what I'm working on now—my mother, my sister, my mother-in-law, my aunts and cousins, and my dear friends—thank you.

To those who have shared your knowledge through all the ways I've absorbed your words and learned how to make things—safely and with some design skills. Alan Revere, Christine Dhein, Celie Fago, Donna Kato, and so many others I've spent time with—thank you.

To my editor and friend, Karla. When the time was right, she asked and supported me every step of the way to bring this book to life. Thank you. Here's to the next one!